W9-CAM-285

History–Social Science Content Standards for California Public Schools reproduced by permission, California Department of Education, CDE Press, 1430 N Street, Suite 3207, Sacramento, CA 95814.

This book
is the property of . . .

State	_____
Province	_____
County	_____
Parish	_____
School District	_____
Other	_____

| Issued To | Year | CONDITION | |
		issued	returned
_____			
_____			
_____			
_____			
_____			
_____			
_____			
_____			
_____			

[_____]

Enter information
in spaces to the left
as instructed

1. Teachers should see that the pupil's name is clearly written in ink in the spaces above in every book issued.
2. The following terms should be used in recording the condition of the book: New; Good; Fair; Poor; Bad.

Pupils to whom this textbook is issued must not write on any page or mark any part of it in any way, consumable textbooks excepted.

THE ANCIENT
SOUTH ASIAN
WORLD

**RONALD MELLOR &
AMANDA H. PODANY**
GENERAL EDITORS

THE ANCIENT SOUTH ASIAN WORLD

*Jonathan Mark Kenoyer
& Kimberley Heuston*

OXFORD
UNIVERSITY PRESS

*To my parents, Marleah June Kenoyer and Quentin Delbert Kenoyer,
for their wonderful example as teachers— J.M.K.*

For Waterford's South Asian students—past, present, and future—with love— K.B.H.

OXFORD
UNIVERSITY PRESS

Oxford University Press, Inc., publishes works
that further Oxford University's objective of excellence
in research, scholarship, and education.

Oxford   New York
Auckland   Cape Town   Dar es Salaam   Hong Kong   Karachi
Kuala Lumpur   Madrid   Melbourne   Mexico City   Nairobi
New Delhi   Shanghai   Taipei   Toronto

With offices in
Argentina   Austria   Brazil   Chile   Czech Republic   France   Greece
Guatemala   Hungary   Italy   Japan Poland   Portugal   Singapore
South Korea   Switzerland   Thailand   Turkey   Ukraine   Vietnam

Copyright © 2005 by Oxford University Press, Inc.
Text copyright © 2005 by Jonathan Mark Kenoyer and Kimberley Heuston

Published by Oxford University Press, Inc.
198 Madison Avenue, New York, New York 10016
www.oup.com

Oxford is a registered trademark of Oxford University Press

Design: Stephanie Blumenthal
Layout: Amy Henderson
Cover design and logo: Nora Wertz

Library of Congress Cataloging-in-Publication Data
Kenoyer, Jonathan M.
The ancient South Asian world / Jonathan Mark Kenoyer & Kimberley Heuston.
p. cm. — (The world in ancient times)
Includes bibliographical references and index.
ISBN-10: 0-19-517422-4 — 0-19-522243-1 (Calif. ed.) — 0-19-522242-3 (9-vol. set)
ISBN-13: 978-0-19-517422-9 — 978-0-19-522243-2 — (Calif. ed.) 978-0-19-522243-2 (9-vol. set)
1. South Asia—Civilization. 2. South Asia—Antiquities.
I. Heuston, Kimberley Burton, 1960- II. Title. III. Series.
DS339.K46 2005
2004020709

Printing number: 9 8 7 6 5 4 3 2 1

Printed in the United States of America on acid-free paper

On the cover: The bull figurine from 2600–1900 BCE was found in Harappa.
Frontispiece: The Buddha achieves enlightenment on this sculpture depicting scenes from his life.

**RONALD MELLOR &
AMANDA H. PODANY**

GENERAL EDITORS

DIANE L. BROOKS, Ed.D.

EDUCATION CONSULTANT

The Early Human World
Peter Robertshaw & Jill Rubalcaba

The Ancient Near Eastern World
Amanda H. Podany & Marni McGee

The Ancient Egyptian World
Eric H. Cline & Jill Rubalcaba

The Ancient South Asian World
Jonathan Mark Kenoyer & Kimberley Heuston

The Ancient Chinese World
Terry Kleeman & Tracy Barrett

The Ancient Greek World
Jennifer T. Roberts & Tracy Barrett

The Ancient Roman World
Ronald Mellor & Marni McGee

The Ancient American World
William Fash & Mary E. Lyons

The World in Ancient Times:
Primary Sources and Reference Volume
Ronald Mellor & Amanda H. Podany

CONTENTS

A 🔲 *marks each chapter's primary sources—ancient writings and artifacts that "speak" to us from the past.*

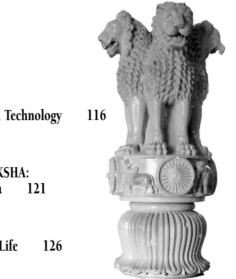

CAST OF CHARACTERS

Because The World in Ancient Times *covers many cultures, we use the abbreviations* BCE *for "Before the Common Era" and* CE *for "Common Era." The traditional equivalents are* BC *for "Before Christ" and* AD *for "Anno Domini," Latin for "In the Year of Our Lord," referring to the birth of Jesus Christ.*

Alexander the Great, 356–323 BCE • Macedonian Greek ruler who conquered Egypt, Persia, and northern India

Ambhi (AHM-bhi), fourth century BCE • King of Taxila, ally of Alexander the Great, and opponent of King Porus

Arjuna (AHR-jun) • Legendary warrior prince who is the hero of the *Bhagavad Gita*

Aryabhata (AHR-yuah-BHUH-tuh), 476–550 CE • India's greatest ancient scientist and author of the *Aryabhatiyam*

Ashoka (uh-SHOK-uh), reigned 269–232 BCE • Greatest of the Mauryan emperors; made Buddhism popular

Bharata (BHAH-ruh-tuh) • Rama's half brother who ruled in Rama's name during his exile

Bindusara (BIN-doo-SAH-rah), reigned 297–277 BCE • Mauryan king; son of Chandragupta and father of Ashoka

Buddha (BOO-dhuh), d. about 420–350 BCE • Born Prince Siddhartha Gautama in what is now Nepal; founder of Buddhism

Chandra Gupta (CHUN-druh GOOP-tuh) **I**, reigned 320–335 CE • Founder of Gupta dynasty; father of Samudra Gupta and grandfather of Chandra Gupta II

Chandra Gupta (CHUN-druh GOOP-tuh) **II**, reigned 376–415 CE • Greatest ruler of the Gupta era, a time when the arts flourished in India

Chandragupta Maurya (CHUN-druh-GOOP-tuh MAOW-ryuh), reigned 321–297 BCE • One of India's great leaders; founder of the Mauryan dynasty

Cyrus the Great, 585–529 BCE • Founder of the Achaemenid dynasty of Persia; conquered parts of Afghanistan and the Indus Valley

Darius I (DAHR-yuhs), 521–486 BCE • Achaemenid emperor who extended his power to the Indus and set up his regional capital at the ancient Vedic city of Taxila

Draupadi (DRAOW-puh-dee) • Legendary wife of Arjuna and his four brothers

Fa-Hien (fah-HYEN) • Chinese pilgrim who visited India to collect Buddhist scriptures in 405–411 CE

Firdausi (fir-DOW-see), 935–1020 CE • Persian poet who compiled accounts of Alexander the Great

Gautama, Siddhartha (GOW-tum-uh, si-DAHR-thuh) • *see* Buddha

Hanuman (HUH-noo-mahn) • Monkey king in the *Ramayana* who helps Rama recover Sita; later worshipped as a god

Kaikeyi (kai-KAY-ee) • Rama's stepmother and one of the villains of the *Ramayana*

Kalidasa (KAH-li-DAH-suh) fifth and sixth centuries CE • Great poet and writer of Gupta era

Kanishka (kuh-NISH-kuh), first century CE • King of the Kushana who briefly united the northern subcontinent

Kannaki (KUH-nuh-kee) • Fictional wife in "The Ankle Bracelet"

Kashyapa (kuh-SHYUH-puh) • Mythical sage who saved the Nagas from the demons of Satisar Lake

Kauravas (KAOW-ruh-vuhs) • 100 brothers whose war with their cousins, the Pandavas, is described in the *Mahabharata*

Kautilya (kaow-TIL-yuh), fourth century BCE • Chandragupta Maurya's great political adviser, author of the *Arthashastra*

Ketu (KEY-tu) short for Shvetaketu (shvey-tuh-KEY-tu), a Brahmin boy mentioned in the *Upanishads* (composed 600–500 BCE) who becomes a philosopher

Kovalan (KOH-vuh-luhn) • Fictional husband in "The Ankle Bracelet"

Mahavira Vardamana (muh-hah-VEE-ruh vuhr-duh-MAH-nuh), sixth century BCE • Founder of the Jain religion; taught the importance of living simply and practicing nonviolence

Manu (MUH-noo) • Mythical author of the Laws of Manu

Muhammad (muh-HAH-mudh), 580–632 CE • Prophet of Islam; born in Arabia

Pandavas (PAHN-duhv or PAHN-duh-vuh) • Five brothers whose war with their cousins, the Kauravas, is told in the *Mahabharata*

Porus (POHR-us), fourth century BCE • King in the Punjab and opponent of Alexander the Great

Puabi (poo-AH-bee), about 2500 BCE • Queen of Ur who was buried with incredible wealth, including beads from the Indus region

Rama (RAHM-uh) • Hero of the *Ramayana*; believed to be a form of the god Vishnu

Rama Gupta (RAHM-uh GOOP-tuh), reigned 376 CE • Cowardly son of Samudra Gupta

Ravana (RAH-vuh-nuh) • Evil ten-headed demon of the Ramayana who captured Sita

Samudra Gupta (suh-MOO-druh GOOP-tuh), reigned 335–376 CE • Gupta emperor and brilliant military leader

Skanda Gupta (SKUHN-duh GOOP-tuh) reigned 455–467 CE • Gupta emperor who defeats the first Hun invaders

Siddhartha • *see* Buddha

Sita (SEE-tah) • Rama's wife, heroine of the *Ramayana*

Valmiki (vahl-MEE-kee), fourth century BCE • Author of the most widely used version of the *Ramayana*

Xuanzang (shwen-dzang), 602–648 CE • Chinese Buddhist monk who traveled to India and wrote *A Record of the Western Regions*

SOME PRONUNCIATIONS

Baluchistan (buh-LOO-chih-stahn)
Dholavira (dho-lah-VEER-rah)
Dilmun (DIL-moon)
Euphrates (yoo-FRAY-teez) River
Ganga River (guhn-GAH)
Gujarat (goo-juh-RAHT)
Gulf of Khambhat (khuhm-BHAHT)
Harappa (huh-RAH-puh)
Hastinapura (huh-STEE-nah-poo-RAH)
Kabul (KAH-bul)
Karakoram (kah-rah-KOHR-ahm)
Kashmir (kuhsh-MEER)
Kausambi (kaow-SHAHM-bee)
Kushana (koo-SHAH-nuh)
Magadha (muh-GUHDGH)
Mathura (MUH-thoo-ruh)
Mehrgarh (MAIR-gahr)
Mesopotamia (MES-uh-puh-TAY-mee-uh)
Mohenjo Daro (mo-HEN-jo DAH-ro)
Pataliputra (pah-tuh-lee-POO-trah)
Persepolis (per-SEP-uh-lus)
Prayaga (pruh-YAHG)
Punjab (puhn-JAHB)
Sravasti (SRAH-vuhs-tee)
Tamralipti (tahm-rah-LIP-tee)
Taxila (tuhk-SHI-lah)
Tigris River (TIE-griss)
Ujjain (ooj-JAHYN)
Vindhya (VIN-dhyuh)
Yamuna River (yuh-MOO-nah)

Over the last 100 million years or so, the landmass that we call India has been sliding toward the much larger Eurasian plate, which includes Europe, Russia, and China. When India ran into Eurasia about 10 million years ago, the site of the collision crumpled into the world's tallest fender bender, three ranges of mountains that are called the Himalaya, the Karakorum, and the Hindu Kush. Today the area south of these spectacular mountains is known as South Asia. As is often the case with ancient civilizations, scholars disagree about exact locations, as with, for example, the lost city of Magan.

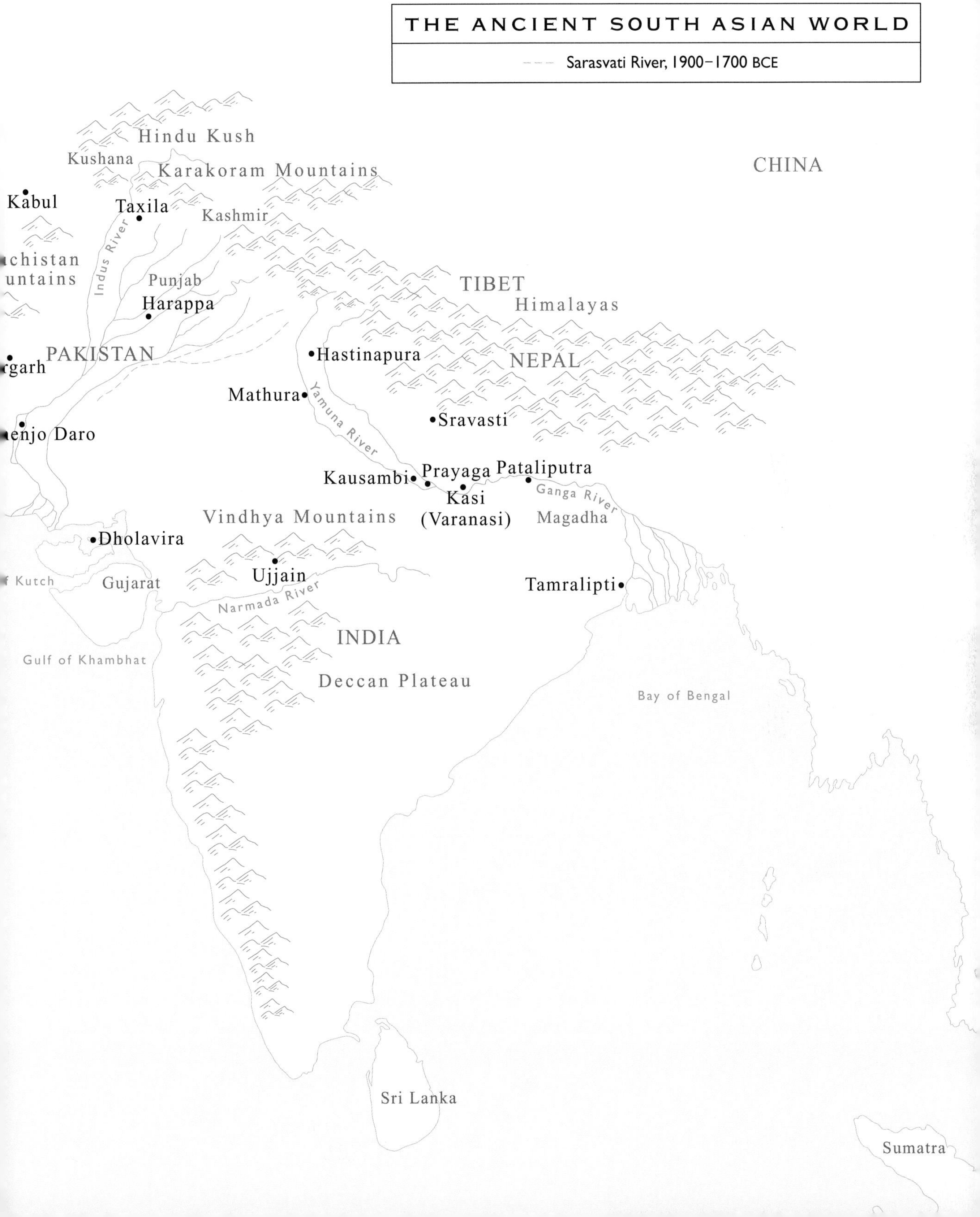

THE ANCIENT SOUTH ASIAN WORLD

---- Sarasvati River, 1900–1700 BCE

Hindu Kush

Kushana

Karakoram Mountains

CHINA

Kabul

Taxila

Kashmir

chistan
untains

Indus River

Punjab

TIBET

Himalayas

Harappa

PAKISTAN

Hastinapura

NEPAL

garh

Mathura

Yamuna River

Sravasti

enjo Daro

Kausambi

Prayaga

Pataliputra

Vindhya Mountains

Kasi
(Varanasi)

Ganga River

Magadha

Dholavira

Kutch

Gujarat

Ujjain

Tamralipti

Narmada River

INDIA

Gulf of Khambhat

Deccan Plateau

Bay of Bengal

Sri Lanka

Sumatra

INTRODUCTION
BEADS IN THE BACKYARD

Jamil Bhatti, a school teacher in Shorkot, Pakistan, sits behind part of his collection of pottery and beads. Mr. Bhatti hopes to open a museum to display the treasures he has found.

Ever since he was a little boy, Jamil Bhatti has enjoyed poking around abandoned lots in the mound on which his city is built. He finds the same kinds of things found in abandoned lots all over the world: broken jars, a scrap of writing, a game piece, a lost earring. Sometimes, if he's lucky, he finds a coin or two.

But the things that Mr. Bhatti finds are older than things most people find lying around their backyards—a lot older. Mr. Bhatti lives in Shorkot, a small city in Pakistan. Some of the backyards in Shorkot have been collecting odds and ends for thousands of years.

When Mr. Bhatti finds something interesting, he brings it home. The children in his neighborhood know that he is interested in old things, and whenever they find some old coins or beads they bring those to him, too. His living room is full of shelves cluttered with pottery and broken figurines—and beads. Lots and lots of beads.

Mr. Bhatti knows what these objects feel and smell like, and the taste they leave on his hands. He knows every inch of the places where they lay buried for so many years, the way the countryside first bakes under the sun, then drowns in the summer rains, and is finally scoured by the freezing winter winds. But sometimes he would like to know more. So he has made a point of getting to know archaeologists who sometimes visit his city. Mr. Bhatti shows the archaeologists the things he has found, and together they talk about what these objects might be, when they were made, and who might have made them.

Archaeologists estimate that Mr. Bhatti's oldest beads were made more than 4,000 years ago, during the time of the Indus Valley civilization. South Asia's first towns and cities grew up during this civilization, which lasted from about 2600 to 1900 BCE. These beads are made of carnelian, a red-orange stone, and lapis lazuli, a bright blue stone. And yet, there are no carnelian or lapis lazuli mines near Shorkot. Carnelian comes from Gujarat, a region of India near the Arabian Sea, 500 miles to the southwest. Lapis

" Carnelian, Khambhat, India, 30,000,000 years ago

" Lapis lazuli bead, Shorkot, Pakistan, 600–300 BCE

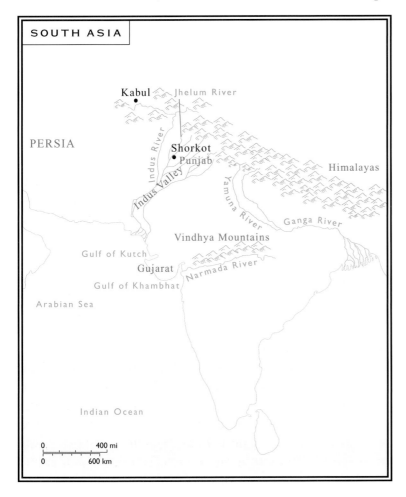

SOUTH ASIA

Kabul
Jhelum River
PERSIA
Indus River
Shorkot
Punjab
Indus Valley
Himalayas
Yamuna River
Ganga River
Vindhya Mountains
Gulf of Kutch
Gujarat
Narmada River
Gulf of Khambhat
Arabian Sea

Indian Ocean

0   400 mi
0   600 km

lazuli comes from the mountains of Northern Afghanistan, 500 miles to the northwest. How did they get to Shorkot?

Traders brought the beads in their packs, carried by foot or camel or boat between the cities of South Asia. Of course these merchants traded more than the precious stones and metals that were sometimes made into beads; grain, wool, and animals were probably the most common goods for sale. Over the thousands of years between then and now, the grain, wool, and animal remains have rotted away, but the polished stone and metal of the beads are still nearly as bright and beautiful as on the day they were made.

Sometime around 1500 BCE, traders stopped traveling through the Punjab (the area of northwestern India and Pakistan surrounding the Indus River). Its cities became smaller or were even abandoned. No one knows why this happened. What we do know is that shortly after the decline of the Indus Valley civilization, new communities with different cultures began to develop in settlements in the northern parts of the **subcontinent**. During this period, many of the stone beads popular as ornaments during the Indus period continued to be made and used, but black and deep red glass beads created in fire became more common.

By about 600 BCE, new cities sprang up in the Punjab and to the east to the area along the Yamuna and Ganga Rivers. A period of peace followed, and it became safe for traders to travel between cities. Bead manufacturers imported black-and white-striped agates, the stones once used to make marbles, from as far away as the Vindhya Mountains in central India. They became more skilled and began to brush black-and-white designs onto their beads. They also donated them to monks, who used shell, crystal, and garnet beads as prayer beads to help them in their meditations and prayers.

Between 558 and 529 BCE, Cyrus the Great of Persia (a large empire to the west of India) conquered parts of Afghanistan, the northern Indus Valley and the Punjab. He and his successors collected tribute, a heavy yearly tax, and sent

sub = "below" in Latin. South Asia lies below the continent of Asia and is divided from the rest of Asia by the Himalayas.

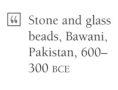

Stone and glass beads, Bawani, Pakistan, 600–300 BCE

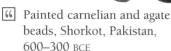

Painted carnelian and agate beads, Shorkot, Pakistan, 600–300 BCE

South Asian monks often use prayer beads to help them meditate and pray. Each bead can represent a prayer or name of a god. They also collect beads from the sacred pilgrimage places and make them into necklaces.

BEADED HISTORY

2600–1900 BCE
Heavy trading of stone and metal beads, grain, wool, and animals within South Asia

About 1500–800 BCE
Growth of new communities in north; black and deep red glass beads created in fire become common

600–500 BCE
Painted carnelian beads and prayer beads become common

550–326 BCE
Mediterranean glass beads arrive from the west

550 BCE to 200 CE
Crystal and amethyst beads traded to Greeks and Romans

officials as well as troops to defend their forts. Some of the multicolored glass beads found at Shorkot are similar to multicolored beads from Greece and other countries bordering the Mediterranean Sea. They were probably brought to South Asia by Persian traders and Greek soldiers hired to fight for the Persians in the Punjab.

When the heroic Macedonian Greek general Alexander the Great and his armies defeated the Persian Empire in 326 BCE, they took over Persian territories in Afghanistan and northwest Pakistan. During their return to Greece, Alexander and his men traveled through the Punjab to the Indus River and probably passed right by Shorkot. Fragments of Greek-style figurines and coins may indicate that some of Alexander's soldiers settled at the site.

By 200 CE, Indian trade networks extended from the Roman Empire to the west, Tibet and China to the north and east, Burma, Thailand, and Southeast Asia to the east and southeast, and Arabia and West Africa to the southwest. Not surprisingly, the beads with white designs from this period in Shorkot turn up not only in the Punjab, but for the first time can be found in all parts of the South Asian subcontinent, as well as China and Southeast Asia.

As Mr. Bhatti gently runs his fingers across his strings of beads, he is touching thousands of years of South Asia's history. From the lapis lazuli and carnelian the people of the Indus Valley imported, to the glass beads and prayer beads of the northern communities and the multicolored glass beads and coins of the Greeks and Persians, his beads tell the story of a rich, complicated, colorful history that happened right in his own backyard. Someday, Mr. Bhatti hopes to establish a museum to share the wonderful history of the city he loves.

A VERY OLD COLLECTION

Archaeologists found a small terracotta pot on the floor of a room that was used for cooking. The pot was filled with dirt, but as the archaeologists began to probe the surface with a pointed piece of bamboo, they dislodged a carnelian bead. Every night for three months, one of the archaeologists carefully excavated the pot, stopping to investigate each new bead. The team members had a contest to see if anyone could guess how many beads were in the pot, but no one was even close.

They finally discovered 133 beads and fragments of stone and copper. The larger beads were on the top and lots of tiny beads were at the very bottom. The beads are all different ages and were probably collected from eroding areas of the site by a child over 3,700 years ago, just like Mr. Bhatti and the children in his neighborhood collect things today.

CHAPTER 1

MOUNTAINS AND MONSOONS

THE GEOGRAPHY OF SOUTH ASIA

For thousands of years, the people of Gujarat, an Indian region that borders the Arabian Sea, have mined chalcedony, a kind of pale gray-blue quartz. Whole families pitch in to work the stone that the miners quarry. Imagine a typical girl in such a family living in Khambhat, a small city in Gujarat, today. We'll call her Mani (pronounced "money"). It's a common name in Khambhat, and it means "jewel."

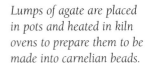

Lumps of agate are placed in pots and heated in kiln ovens to prepare them to be made into carnelian beads.

Miners dig pebbles of chalcedony out of deep pits. These lumps of stone are too hard for ordinary tools to shape, so Mani's family leaves them to dry in the sun and then bakes them to make them more brittle and easy to chip into smaller pieces. They put the lumps of rock in earthenware pots that they arrange in a fire pit and then cover with cheap, flammable fuel such as sawdust, rice husks, or dried cow-dung chips. After the fire is lit, Mani helps her father cover the pit with a sheet of iron so nothing can fall into the fire. The pots are left there for a couple of days, until the fire burns out, the ash cools, and the pale chalcedony has been transformed into bright red carnelian.

Mani and her brothers and sisters chip and split the lumps of carnelian into smaller pieces. Then they grind and polish them with an electric grinding wheel. Once they are about the right size, Mani takes the beads to another family whose father drills holes in the beads. After being drilled, the beads are tumbled in a polishing drum with a little water and emery dust (a hard, gritty substance that is sometimes used on nail files) until they are smooth and shiny. Except

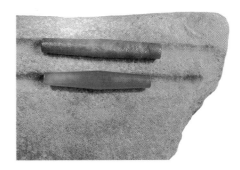

❝ Bead-grinding stone with beads, Chanhu Daro, Pakistan, 2600–1900 BCE

Monsoons are welcomed across South Asia, as they end the dry season. But the rains and winds also cause floods and destroy crops.

"Monsoon" comes from the Arabic word *mausim*, which means "season." Monsoons blow rain inland from the southwest between May and September, and generate winds from the northeast between October and April.

for the electric grinders and polishers, the same tools have been used to make beads like these for thousands of years.

Mani's whole family helps make beads, but it is not their only work. They have a farm, just like most Indian families who live outside large cities. They work on the beads during their free time, mostly the winter and spring, to make a little extra money. The piles of stones lie undisturbed in July and August, however. That is when the **monsoons** come.

Usually when people use the word "sunny," they mean something good. But in South Asia, where summer temperatures can get higher than 115° F, dark clouds symbolize happiness. The entire country holds its breath in June, when the earth lies dry and cracked beneath the merciless sun, and the winds are thick with heat and dust. Then, beginning in the south, the clouds build up, and the rain comes.

This is no ordinary rain. An ancient poem by the Indian writer Valmiki called the *Ramayana* describes it this way:

"Dark clouds, heavily laden, floated along, frequently eclipsing the sun, gradually massing themselves like an army of gigantic elephants; thunders rumbled and shook the trees, ripped off their foliage, and scattered it in the air; scoured the earth and sprayed up mud and dust."

❝ Valmiki, *Ramayana*, 300–200 BCE

It rains and rains, sometimes for weeks at a time. Farming families have no time for anything but planting and cultivating their crops. Mani and her family fall into bed at night, drenched and exhausted, with no time even to think about the pile of stones waiting in a corner of the courtyard.

People across South Asia dance with joy when the rains come. But after a month of damp skin, flooded houses, and hard work planting muddy fields, they also celebrate when the monsoons leave. Bead making is hard work, too; working with stone leaves Mani's hands bruised and sore, and she sometimes wishes that she lived in the city like her cousins, who have to work in their father's bead shop only after their schoolwork is done.

There was one day, however, when she was glad to be a country girl in Khambhat instead of a jeweler's daughter in Bhuj, a city on the island of Kutch in western Gujarat. On January 26, 2001, India celebrated its 51st anniversary of independence from Great Britain. It was a holiday, so Mani didn't have school. She was in the courtyard, sorting stones before the Independence Day parade started, when the ground began to shake. A minute and a half later, when the earthquake and the screaming were over, many of the modern concrete buildings in the cities in the Gujarat region had collapsed. More than 20,000 people were dead, and more than 600,000 families had lost their homes.

Mani's family was one of the lucky ones. Their house was fine, although it was hard to find clean water and food, and they had no electricity for a long time. But they lived in the country, and made do. Their cousins in Bhuj were not as lucky. They lived in a modern concrete house, which collapsed and took everything they owned.

In 2001, a huge earthquake in Gujarat, India, killed more than 20,000 people and destroyed many of the area's homes, museums, and monuments.

Attack of the Killer Ants

This Greek myth about Indian gold from Arrian's Indika, *written in 150 CE, might be based on some truth. Burrowing animals called marmots dig their dens on the banks of the upper reaches of the Indus River. In some places they dig down to a level that has gold-bearing sand, which ends up at the mouth of their burrows.*

They get the gold from ants . . . [that] are larger than foxes. . . . They dig holes in the earth . . . [and t]he heap which they throw up consists of gold the purest and brightest in all the world. . . . The people arrive at noon, a time when the ants have gone underground, and at once seizing the booty make off at full speed. The ants, on learning what has been done, pursue the fugitives, and overtaking them fight with them till they conquer or die, for of all animals they are the most courageous.

These three parts of South Asian life—the precious stones, and monsoons that enable families like Mani's to make a living, and the earthquake that threatened them—are all connected. The Indian peninsula lies on one tectonic plate, a landmass that floats on the earth's molten core, which is colliding with the larger European and Asian (Eurasian) plate. The extreme pressures and high heat created in the deep layers of the earth's crust make precious metals such as gold and silver as well as colorful crystals such as emeralds, sapphires, rubies, garnets, and diamonds.

Precious stones like lapis lazuli, jade, serpentine and turquoise, as well as metals like copper and tin, are formed in other layers of the earth's crust. As the Indian landmass

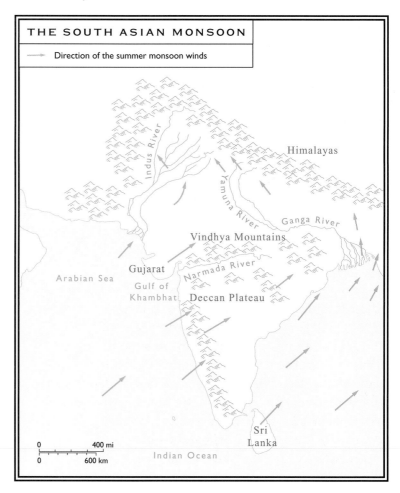

THE SOUTH ASIAN MONSOON

→ Direction of the summer monsoon winds

Himalayas
Indus River
Yamuna River
Ganga River
Vindhya Mountains
Gujarat
Narmada River
Arabian Sea
Gulf of Khambhat
Deccan Plateau
Sri Lanka
Indian Ocean

0   400 mi
0   600 km

crashed against the Eurasian plate millions of years ago, it pushed up the lowest levels of the earth's crust to form the Himalayas, the highest mountains in the world. As the mountains were formed—and they are still growing three to four inches (seven to nine centimeters) a year—the deeply buried layers with valuable metals and rocks were brought up to the surface, where wind and water wear away the earth that covers them.

In the peninsular region, the molten rocks, called lava, escaped through cracks in the crust. As the lava cooled, mineral gases collected and slowly hardened to form chalcedony, a pale gray stone. Chalcedony is harder than the surrounding lava, and over millions of years the softer rock around it wore away, until lumps of chalcedony were washed down the mountains and collected in hollow areas in wide valleys.

Long before there was a city called Khambhat or a region called Gujarat, **Paleolithic** hunter-gatherers collected pieces of chalcedony and chipped them into sharp blades to use for knives, arrow points, and scrapers. By the time of India's first civilization, the Indus civilization of about 2600 BCE, the more settled farmers began to make beads from the chalcedony.

paleo + *lithic* = "old" + "stone" During the Paleolithic period, also called the Old Stone Age, humans used stone tools but they did not farm. The period lasted from about 2 million BCE to 10,000 BCE.

Then as now, people found the beads beautiful and used them as symbols of wealth and power. They were probably used for barter and trade like modern money. A lot of people were buried wearing a few beads, so they may also have been used as amulets, a form of protection from evil. Traders from distant lands came to Gujarat to trade for the stones and eventually many of the beads ended up as far away as Mesopotamia, in present-day Iraq, and the Mediterranean coast. In the days when transportation by boat was faster, simpler, and safer than journeys overland, the Narmada River was the best way to get into India's interior. What's more, protected bays along the coasts of India made it possible to anchor boats large enough to make the sea journey to far away places such as Arabia, Africa, Sri Lanka, and eventually to Southeast Asia and China.

People do not live by beads—or even trade—alone. They also need a dependable food supply. Fortunately for the South

Basalt is a dark-colored
volcanic rock.

The Deccan plateau is made
of very old volcanic rock and
is the middle part of the
South Asian subcontinent,
south of the Indus and Ganga
River valleys. (A plateau is a
flat region that is higher than
the surrounding land.)

Asians, over millions of years, the monsoon rains and hot sun eroded the rocks of the Himalaya Mountains to create the fertile soil of the Indus and Ganges River valleys. These areas are watered by the annual monsoons and also by the rivers. The farmers in the Indus and Ganges plant crops such as wheat, barley, and rice, which require lots of water and regular rainfall.

In western and central India, where the monsoons are not as strong, a fine black soil created from soft **basalt** rock helps farming. This soil is especially precious because even when there is only a little rainfall, it can soak up a lot of water and store it for months at a time. In Gujarat and central India, farming communities grow crops such as millet and sorghum, which are cereal grains that grow well in this type of soil. In some regions it is called "black cotton soil," because cotton grows so well in it.

In the late spring and early summer, a wind begins to blow from the southwest. This wind, the monsoon, brings rain clouds from the Indian Ocean. When these winds and clouds hit land, they dump their first heavy rainfall, making a lush tropical forest that is perfect for growing trees like mahogany and teak, as well as spices such as pepper, nutmeg, cardamom, and ginger.

The now lighter clouds get blown far to the east, leaving much less rainfall in the central **Deccan plateau**. In time they start piling up against the high mountains of the eastern Himalaya, where they begin dumping large quantities of rain. When the winds blow in the opposite direction during the winter monsoon, they pick up a little moisture from the snow-covered mountains and drop a little rain in central India before reaching the Indian Ocean once again.

By the sixth century BCE, sailors had learned that they could go from Sri Lanka to what is now called Indonesia and Thailand using the southwest winds of the summer monsoon. In the winter, when the winds come from the north and east, they could sail back to Sri Lanka. Or, they could use the winter winds to go to the Maldive Islands, in the Arabian Sea, and then on to East Africa or south to Madagascar. As early as 2600 BCE, sailors used a route that

ran from Gujarat to Oman and the Persian Gulf. When the summer monsoon began, the sailors headed home, coming back in time for the long rainy season that filled the rivers and streams and watered the lush jungles and forests of the subcontinent.

Trying to sum up all of South Asia's different regions—the jungles of the river valleys, the towering mountains in the north, the vast plateaus and deserts of the south—is a lot like the old Indian tale of blind men trying to describe an elephant. The first man feels the elephant's trunk, and says, "An elephant is like a snake." The second feels the elephant's body, and says, "It's not at all like a snake! It's like a wall." The third, who is feeling the tail, thinks both of them are crazy. He knows an elephant is like a rope. Throughout South Asia's long history, billions of people have loved South Asia and called it home. But no one story, no one book, not even one whole lifetime is big enough to learn all of this dramatic land's secrets.

The Indus River flows down from the high Himalayan mountains, bringing water and fertile silt to the land along its banks. South Asia's first civilization grew up along the banks of the Indus.

CHAPTER 2

66 HAND AXE IN
KASHMIR, STONE
TOOL IN PAKISTAN,
AND SANSKRIT
LEGEND

STONE SERPENTS
EARLY HUMANS AND STONE AGE CULTURES

In 1969, a young Indian archaeologist, Hasmukh Sankalia, decided to visit Kashmir to take a look at some glacial deposits, mixtures of rocks and pebbles left behind by a melting glacier. He didn't expect to find any sign of early humans—more experienced archaeologists had already looked at the site and thought it so unimportant that they left and went sightseeing instead. But Dr. Sankalia had never seen that particular kind of glacial deposit before, and he studied each bit of earth and lump of stone, trying to find a trace of the glacier. In his autobiography he writes:

> One curious-looking stone I kept, as a child would keep a fine glossy pebble found on a river bank or a sea shore. It definitely showed some ice action. Lo, and behold, the next moment, my eyes fell upon the wavy edge of a large broken greyish stone. The rest of the stone was inside the section [ground], so we were not sure whether it was a tool—a man-made thing or just a broken piece of stone. Not expecting any tool, I took it out though normally we photograph the object before its removal. To my great joy and surprise the flake bore all the signs of a man-made tool.

Later, Dr. Sankalia would find a hand axe in the same area. This time, he was careful to take a photograph of the object *before* removing it from the ground.

Why was he so excited by his discovery? Because the tool was the same shape as tools that archaeologists had found in other parts of India and Africa that dated from about 400,000 BCE. No one had ever found evidence of early

Archaeologists Robin Dennell (foreground) and Linda Hurcombe and geologist Imran Khan search for ancient stone tools and fossils in the Pabbi Hills, near Riwat, Pakistan.

66 Hand axe, Kashmir, 400,000 BCE

Archaeologists often draw their finds to help them see the way they were shaped by ancient humans. The curved lines in this drawing of a hand axe indicate the direction from which a hammer stone hit the rock to shape the tool, like a ripple caused by a stone thrown into a pond.

human remains that old in Kashmir before. This discovery, and more recent finds in Riwat, Pakistan show that humans had lived in many parts of Asia much earlier than scholars had previously thought.

Ten years later another team of archaeologists along with geologists, scientists who study the history of landforms, confirmed Dr. Sankalia's discovery. They said that other rocks and fossils at the site where Dr. Sankalia found the tool also dated from 400,000 BCE. The geologists explained that at one time the entire region of Kashmir had been a huge lake that formed 4,000,000 years ago as the Indian subcontinent crashed into Asia. Because the mountains around the lake were so high, melting ice and rain collected in the lake without a way out.

About 400,000 years ago, earthquakes tilted up one side of the valley so that the lake moved and exposed new land. The stone tool was made by someone who hunted for food in the newly exposed land next to the deep, dark lake. More earthquakes cracked the mountain ranges about 200,000 years ago, and the water began to escape and form the Jhelum River, shrinking the lake further.

Winters in this valley were hard—too cold, windy, and snowy for early humans to survive. In the beginning, people hunted in the valley during the summer and moved back to the plains in the winter. Finally, in about 10,000 BCE, the climate warmed, the glaciers melted, and humans could live on the land all year long. The only remains of the once mighty lake that covered all of Kashmir are small lakes such as Nagin Lake, the "Lake of the Serpents."

Nagin Lake is named after "Nagas," legendary serpent-like beings who are believed to live near lakes and springs. These Nagas, who are worshiped to this day, are supposed to have the power to make the soil fertile and protect humans from evil spirits.

The legend of the Nagas is very old. Even before they could write, ancient people remembered important things by telling stories, singing songs, and drawing pictures about them. Their storytellers became good at memorizing things, able to remember the equivalent of thousands of pages of

Stone tool, Riwat, Pakistan, 2 million years ago

KASHMIR'S CREATION

4 million years ago
Mountains push up, blocking the rivers to create a lake

400,000 years ago
Earthquakes move lake covering Kashmir; early humans hunt with stone tools on exposed land

200,000 years ago
Earthquakes create Jhelum River, drain Kashmir lake

10,000 years ago
Glaciers melt; Nagin Lake and small lakes form; humans settle in Kashmir year-round

500–600 CE
Epic of *Nilmata Purana* written

written text. Some of their legends and hymns were passed on for thousands of years before they were finally written down in the ancient Indian language of Sanskrit. The legend of the Nagas is found in the *Nilmata Purana*. Legends from the *Nilmata Purana* were at least 1,000 years old, and maybe much older, before they were finally written down in about 500–600 CE.

According to the *Nilmata Purana*, Kashmir was first settled by people who were called "Nagas." They lived around the springs that fed Satisaras, the Sea of the Goddess (an ancient lake in the valley of modern Kashmir). Unfortunately for the Nagas, the evil demon Jalodbhava and his black-hearted henchmen also lived in the Satisaras. From time to time, the demons emerged from Satisaras's murky waters and fed on the Nagas. After many years of suffering, the Nagas prayed to the gods for help. The gods heard their pleas and sent the wise man Kashyapa to help the Nagas.

Kashyapa asked the gods to stop the demons from eating the Nagas, so they all gathered together, headed by the

> 66 *Nilmata Purana,* about 500–600 CE

HOW OLD IS IT?

One simple but effective way of figuring out how old something is, is to compare it with things whose ages we *do* know. For example, if a pot of a certain design is buried with some charcoal, scientists can use atomic analysis to figure out how long ago the charcoal was burned. If it was burned 5,000 years ago, it's reasonable to assume that the pot, which cannot be analyzed in the same way, is about 5,000 years old. It's also reasonable to assume that other pots with the same design are also about 5,000 years old, even if they were not buried in exactly the same place.

Boulders along the Indus River at Chilas, Pakistan, are covered with sunburst designs, animals, and armed warriors. These petroglyphs, which mean "stone pictures" in Greek, were carved by travelers and hunters over thousands of years, between 3000 BCE and 400 CE.

The Nagas were mythological serpentlike beings that lived near springs and lakes. This modern stone cobra was carved for worshippers to place on a shrine to honor the Nagas.

supreme god Brahma. Jalodbhava fled back to the depths of the lake where he was invincible, and the gods were left sitting on the mountain tops trying to figure out how to destroy him. Finally, the god Vishnu decided to call his brother Balabhadra, who had a magical weapon in the form of a gigantic plough. Using the tip of the plow, he cut through the mountain and drained the water from the lake. After the lake was drained, the demon Jhalodbhava lost his power, and the god Vishnu swooped down from the heavens to finish him off. Then Kashyapa settled his people on the fertile land that had been a lake bed.

But the Naga's troubles weren't over. They had angered Kashyapa, and he cursed the land so that it could only be used six months a year for four long ages. After the ages had passed, the Nagas and other people were finally free to live on the land throughout the year.

What are we to make of this story? Who could have composed it? And how could they have possibly known about the prehistoric history of the region? That is an unanswered question, the kind of puzzle that scholars hope to be able to solve one day.

CHAPTER 3

FARMERS AND HERDERS
NEOLITHIC TIMES

Domesticate comes from *domus*, the Latin word for "home." To domesticate animals is to make them feel at home, to accustom them to living close to humans, to tame them.

During the Neolithic period, also called the New Stone Age, the first farmers used stone tools to raise crops. In South Asia, the period lasted from 7000 BCE to 5500 BCE.

About 9,000 years ago, a new way of life began to spread throughout regions of South Asia. Instead of wandering around the countryside hunting animals and gathering wild plants for food, people began to stay in one place. By planting crops and **domesticating** animals, they didn't have to follow their food anymore.

These people couldn't write, so we don't have any written records to tell us their story. But they left enough of their stuff behind—houses, tools, weapons, and even garbage—that historians today can figure out quite a bit about their daily lives.

Say a historian was considering the life of a young girl who lived in Mehrgarh, a village that is now an archaeological site in Pakistan, in about 7000 BCE. We'll give her the name Jana. Animal bones, including horns that are smaller than those found on wild animals, tell us that Jana and her family most likely made their living by herding sheep, cattle, and goats.

Each May, once the mountain passes were dry enough to cross on foot, Jana and her family left their village for the mountains, where there was more grass for their animals to eat. In the winter, it was too cold for **Neolithic** people to survive in the mountains with their herds. Archaeologists have found evidence of camps in the mountains that used exactly the same kinds of stone tools as the villages below, so it could be that the same people lived in both places.

After a week of travel, Jana's family would have reached their camp. The boys and some of the men probably continued on to higher pastures to fatten the herds with sweet mountain grass, as they do today. Jana stayed in the summer camp, spinning wool and cotton, weaving storage bags, and making finely woven baskets from the willows that grew along the mountain streams. Although archaeologists

have not found any bags, which would have rotted away by now, they have found tools made out of shell that were used for spinning. Since women today use spun wool to weave bags, it seems likely that they did the same then. Archaeologists *have* found evidence of woven baskets in grave sites. These baskets were waterproofed with a coating of bitumen, a natural form of tar that Jana could have collected on her way up the Bolan River valley.

In late August, the boys returned from the high pastures and announced that the fields of wild wheat and barley were ready to be harvested. Archaeologists would later find impressions of these wild grains left in mud bricks. Jana got busy making stone blades out of chert, a hard stone that flakes easily. She would have attached these blades to a wooden handle with bits of sticky bitumen to make a sickle, a curved tool for cutting grasses.

After three weeks of hard work, all the bags Jana and the other women had spent the summer weaving were filled with

Bitumen-coated basket, Mehrgarh, Pakistan, 7000–6000 BCE

Sickle, Mehrgarh, Pakistan, 6000 BCE

The sharp stone blades and bitumen glue are all that's left of this ancient sickle, which was used for cutting grasses.

wild grain. Everyone helped carry the bulging supply of winter food down the mountain, even the animals. The sheep and goats were loaded with small saddlebags that weighed about 25 pounds, while the bullocks could carry about 150 pounds. The trip home would have been made in slow and easy stages, so the animals had plenty of time to graze and stay nice and fat.

Archaeologists assume that the domesticated animals were used as pack animals, but there is no easy way to test this. Since modern nomads use woven bags to carry their belongings on pack animals, historians assume by **analogy** that the earlier people did things about the same way. They estimate the weight of the bags by measuring the weight those animals can comfortably carry.

Some of the members of Jana's village did not make the long trip into the mountains. They stayed home and experimented with new kinds of wheat and barley they got from traders from the west. Let's say Jana's aunt and uncle were among the people who decided to plant crops in the open meadows near the village. These new grains had bigger kernels with a thinner husk, so they were easier to grind into

"Analogy" is from the Greek word *analogos*, meaning proportional. An analogy is a way of understanding something by comparing it to something else that has similar characteristics.

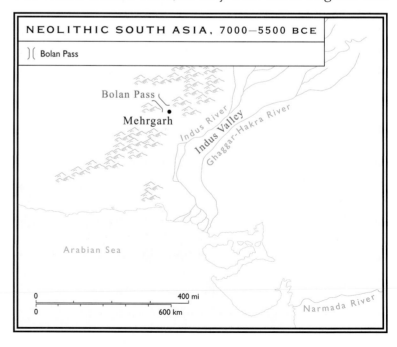

NEOLITHIC SOUTH ASIA, 7000–5500 BCE

)(Bolan Pass

Bolan Pass
Mehrgarh

Indus River
Indus Valley
Ghaggar-Hakra River

Arabian Sea

0   400 mi
0   600 km

Narmada River

flour, and the flat bread they made was less chewy than the old-fashioned kind made with wild wheat.

When Jana's family returned, they probably had to repair their mud-brick home after the storms and floods of the monsoon season. Fortunately, the sturdy mud-brick foundation with its food storage areas usually remained intact. In order to repair the house, they would have dug clay from the river and mixed it with sand and the chaff from the harvested grain to make mud bricks.

After her house was repaired, Jana and her cousins cut away the weeds that had grown up in the fields near their home during the rainy season. Then they burned the field. After it was cleared, they broke up the soil with sticks weighted with ring-shaped stones to make them heavier and more effective. Jana and her cousins dropped seeds into the hollows they had made, and then dug a small channel from the river to help water this first planting. The new varieties of grain required irrigation; rainfall alone did not provide enough moisture for the tender young plants. In a few weeks there would be winter rain that would help water the fields and allow the grain to grow and then ripen.

As soon as the wheat began to sprout a few weeks later, Jana and her cousins would have had the responsibility of keeping the deer and antelope from nibbling the new shoots. Each night, the two of them would have made small fires at the corners of the field. One of them would have tended the fire, while the other would have sat on a small platform with a good view of the whole field and a pile of clay balls that had been baked in the fire. Whenever a deer or an antelope got too close, Jana or her cousin would have put a ball in a sling and flung it at the intruder. Although this sounds like a fun job, it was not. Children probably would have tried to pass the time by telling stories and singing songs, but the nights seemed very long. There was always a chance that leopards and tigers, hunting the deer and antelope, would not be scared away by the fires and would come after Jana and her cousins instead.

During the Neolithic period, ancient people didn't just adjust to the world around them. Instead, they began to

NEOLITHIC CUISINE

Neolithic people raised cattle, goats, and sheep for wool and milk, which they drank or made into cheese or yogurt. The people of ancient South Asia also ate fresh and dried fruit, especially dates and jujube, a plumlike fruit used in chutney, a kind of sweet relish. But most of their calories came from barley or wheat.

To cook barley without pottery, put clean sand in a basket and heat it with hot rocks that are pulled from the fire. When the sand is hot, add the barley and slowly roast it until it is golden brown and its seed coverings are loose. After straining the grain, either mix it with water to make a cold porridge or grind it into flour. You can then bake the flour into flat bread or mix it with cold, sweetened water to make *sattu*, a refreshing drink popular in Pakistan and northern India.

HOW TO TURN WOLVES INTO PUPPY DOGS

Because animals with big horns and bad tempers can be dangerous for humans, shepherds choose to breed the smallest, most easy-going animals. That is why domesticated animals are usually gentler than their larger wild cousins. Domesticated animals also tend to produce more milk and have more babies.

On the other hand, if breeders are raising their animals for fighting, racing, food, or ritual sacrifice, they mate their biggest and most aggressive animals. Later communities at Harappa, for example, seem to have bred large sheep, possibly for food or sacrifice to their gods.

change their world to better serve their needs. They experimented with grains and saved seeds that made it easier to plant crops close to their villages, and domesticated the animals they needed to live.

Having a dependable food source in one place allowed them to build better, longer-lasting homes, which, in time, grew into large villages with many families living together. Living in one place also made it possible to develop many different types of crafts, such as pottery making, wood-working, bead making, and house building.

Over time, villagers built walls around their communities to protect them from bandits and wild animals. Many people moved to these central places for protection and to be close to the markets. Anthropologists, scientists who study the history of humankind, call the development of agriculture the "Agricultural Revolution" because it improved the quality of human life so much. It's too bad that the people like Jana who lived through it probably did not understand that their daily, ordinary activities would have such an astonishing effect on the world to come.

Zebu cattle were first raised by the ancient South Asians for use in the hot and often dry plains of the Indus valley. They used them for meat, milk, and especially for pulling carts and plows.

CHAPTER 4

GADGETS GALORE
THE BEGINNINGS OF TECHNOLOGIES AND TRADE

The thought of having to cook dinner at the end of a long day is sometimes almost more than your tired parents can bear—even with the help of grocery stores, refrigerators, and microwave ovens. Imagine what it must have been like in the ancient village of Mehrgarh. Not only was there no fast food, there weren't even any pots or pans. For the village's first 1,500 years, villagers cooked their food, using nothing more than hot stones, baskets, and perhaps leather sacks. Every cook must have wished a hundred times for some kind of vessel that could be put directly over the fire, that could hold water better than a bitumen-coated basket, and that a rat couldn't chew through.

About 5500 BCE, the villagers realized that a solution to the problem of cooking and food storage was right at their feet—the fine, silty mud called clay. They dug it out of its slippery deposits by the river with digging sticks, then pounded it to bits and dried it in the hot sun for a couple of days. Then they sifted it to remove any small rocks or leaves, kneaded it with water until it formed large balls, then covered the balls with a damp cloth. For several days, water seeped into the clay. Then it was finally ready to shape into a pot or a small human or animal figure.

❝ Figurines, Nausharo, Pakistan, 2600 BCE

These painted male figurines wear turbans on their heads and long trousers. The center figure holds an infant and wears an elaborate headdress of the sort usually worn by women.

AND WE DO MEAN TINY

Clay is mostly made up of tiny flat disks of silica and alumina that water and wind have separated from larger rocks. How tiny is tiny? Less than 1/6000 of an inch, or 4 microns, across. In nature, these disks stick together with the help of water, which gives clay a soft, squashy texture. After the water evaporates, the clay gets hard. When hard clay is baked at high temperatures in a special oven called a kiln, the silica begins to melt and the clay becomes almost as hard as a rock.

At first, potters stacked coils of clay on top of each other and pinched and squashed the coils together to make smooth-walled pots. At some point people realized that it would be easier to work on all the sides of a pot if it were on a dish or platter that could be spun around. They also found that adding sand and fine gravel to the clay made pots strong enough to survive cooking fires—no more putting your hand in the flames to retrieve a fallen piece of meat. By about 3500–3300 BCE, potters had discovered that "throwing"—shaping their pots on the fast-turning disks—was faster than the coil method.

The potter's wheel is a large, flat disk with a socket on the bottom that fits over a round spike set in the ground, like a cupped hand over a fist. The first wheels required a lot of strength and skill to spin, but potters had more control with a spinning wheel. They could make pots that were more even and had thinner walls than coil pots. After the potters shaped the pots, they sliced them off the wheels with pieces of thread that they held tightly between their hands. When the pots had dried, artisans coated the inside or outside with slip, finely ground colored clay mixed with water until it was about the thickness of cream. The coating of slip helped to seal all the tiny holes in the clay and make the surface more waterproof. Sometimes artisans would decorate their pots and figures with brushes made from the tail hair of a goat and dipped into red, brown, black, or white slip.

Painted terracotta bowl, Baluchistan, Pakistan, 3300 BCE

This bowl, used as a burial offering, was painted with crushed lapis powder and red ochre. It was stolen from an ancient graveyard by antique collectors.

The next step was to fire the pots, baking the clay so that the pots were stronger and watertight—finally, a way to lug all the water back home without dropping any of it. At first, potters put their pots in bonfires covered with burning brush. Later, potters learned that they could get the firing hotter and the pots stronger if the fire was enclosed in a kiln, a sort of oven. If a potter wanted to make a pot extra special, he or she might paint it with bright paints made from powdered lapis lazuli (a bright blue stone) or malachite (an emerald-green stone). These paints were put on after the pottery had been fired.

Potters made more than pots. They also made small figures that were probably used for praying to the gods, as well as toys for their children. Archaeologists can't always tell the difference between objects meant for sacred rituals and those made to be toys. Today in India, after a mother is finished praying with a clay figurine, she often gives it to her children to play with. Archaeologists have found many broken and thrown-away figurines that may have been used first for rituals and later as toys. Some animal figurines had holes at the bottom to attach wheels and a hole at the top for a pull string, just like the plastic and wooden toys that little kids like to pull around today.

Archaeologists don't know who did what job. Most believe that women made the first coil pots, as they still do in some remote Indian villages. For one thing, women were in charge of cooking, so they were the ones who cared most about making it easier. For another, women probably made the baskets that came before the coiled pots, and their shapes are similar.

But the potter's wheel changed things. It takes a lot of

At Harappa, traditional potters still use a foot-powered wheel to quickly turn large amounts of clay into beautiful pots.

🔍 Ram toys, Harappa, Pakistan, 2600 BCE

strength and regular practice to work the wheel. It's not the kind of job you can do in between chasing your children around, and most women of the ancient world spent much of their time and energy on the important work of raising, feeding, and clothing their families. In many parts of the world, men began to work as full-time potters after the invention of the potter's wheel.

Does that mean that there were no women potters in later times? Probably not. In many regions of South Asia, even though men may throw pottery using the wheel, the women and young girls do most of the clay preparation and fine decoration work.

Not every community lived near riverbed clay deposits, of course, so not every village had its own potter. But they may have had some other precious resource. Young people who lived near the sea, for example, became skilled divers and shell workers. Shell was used to make small tools and ornaments, especially **bangles**.

The word *bangle* comes from the Hindi word *bangri*. A bangle is a round bracelet in the shape of a ring.

❝ Shell bangles, Harappa, Pakistan, 2600 BCE

Ore is rock that contains metal.

People who lived in the Baluchistan Mountains to the west or the Aravalli hills to the east of Indus Valley learned how to work the copper in their soil. At first they collected bits of copper that were already in metal form and pounded them into beads or small pins and knives. They also developed techniques for getting copper from copper **ore**. Metal workers used wood charcoal to make very hot fires that could melt the metal out of the rock. To make the charcoal, people had to cut down forests. Over thousands of years, the copper-producing areas became deforested.

Like shell bangles, stone beads were very common in South Asia, where they were symbols of wealth and power.

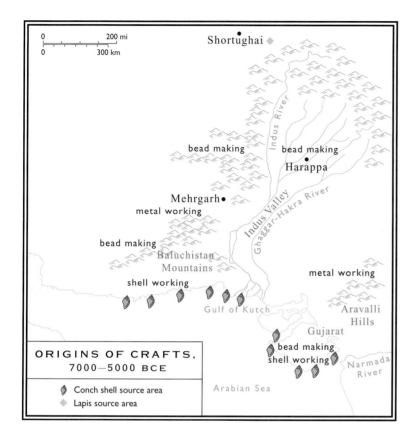

0 | 200 mi
0 | 300 km

Shortughai

bead making   bead making
Harappa

Indus River

Mehrgarh•
metal working

bead making
Baluchistan
Mountains   Ghaggar-Hakra River
Indus Valley

shell working

metal working

Gulf of Kutch   Aravalli
Hills

Gujarat
bead making
shell working   Narmada
River

Arabian Sea

ORIGINS OF CRAFTS,
7000—5000 BCE

Conch shell source area
Lapis source area

The earliest bead makers drilled stone beads of soft lime-stone and soapstone in the highlands of Baluchistan and the deserts of Rajasthan. There were also deposits of chert, a hard stone that is easy to split into sharp-edged tools, and jasper, a kind of quartz, suitable for making drill bits. Later bead makers shaped and drilled other types of stones, such as green serpentine from Baluchistan and blue lapis lazuli from Afghanistan.

In Gujarat and Afghanistan, bead makers chipped, ground, and drilled agates and carnelian. At first, artisans made beads close to the places where the rock was quarried. The artisans would trade them during festivals, when every-one came together at the end of the harvest season. In time, merchants and craftsmen in the villages began to import the raw stone and make the beads locally in villages far from the mining areas. Many of the beads are extremely small,

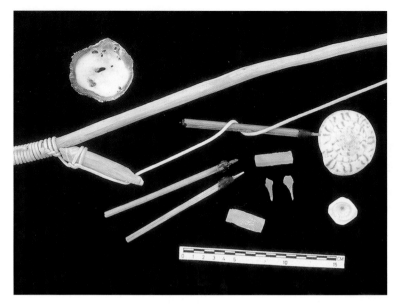

Archaeologists create models of ancient bow drills to learn how long it would have taken ancient people to make holes in shell and stone. This bow drill uses bits made from tiny stone blades.

66 Bead necklace, Mehrgarh, Pakistan, 7000–5500 BCE

and children, who have small and nimble fingers, may have been involved in the grinding and polishing as well as the stringing of the beads.

These finished products—terracotta pots, copper pins, shell jewelry, stone beads—were rare and precious luxuries to people of other regions who didn't have the materials or the technology to make their own. Because there were no malls and shopping centers in ancient South Asia, merchants could profit from trading items from one region to the other, such as shell items from the coast for copper from the highlands.

Villages and towns surrounded by protective walls grew up along the trade routes, usually at important crossroads or in areas with good farmland that could support a lot of people. Craftspeople began to live in these larger villages and towns because they were filled with customers who would buy their products, and the walls protected their workshops. By 2800 BCE, these trading centers would grow into South Asia's first cities, where busy people could buy the things they needed—even dinner.

CHAPTER 5

WALLS AND WELLS
THE FIRST CITIES
OF THE INDUS

Here and there, mysterious mounds 50 feet tall lie scattered across the countryside like a giant's abandoned game of checkers. Even though some of the mounds are huge—as big as hundreds of football fields—there's not much to see. Some crumbling mud bricks. A few tumbled brick walls and some blocks of stone. We are in the Punjab, a quarter of a million square miles of mostly flat, dry farmland. There's nothing worth paying attention to here, unless of course you are an archaeologist, or an engineer who needs some gravel to build a railway.

In the early 1850s, British engineers began to build a railroad through the Punjab. They usually laid the rails on a foundation of crushed rock, but there's not much rock in the Punjab. So the engineers decided to use the old bricks that littered the mounds. An archaeologist named Alexander Cunningham who had been digging in the area tried to stop them. He knew that the mounds covered the remains of ancient civilizations. He was hoping to find evidence of Buddhist times, which began about 500 BCE. But even he couldn't find anything in the ruins that seemed important— just some broken pottery and a few stone tools. And one other thing: a small carved stone seal.

Carved stone seals were common in the ancient world. Merchants and government officials stamped them into soft clay instead of writing a signature. The seals were usually decorated with pictures of animals and sometimes a few signs or symbols. Cunningham's seal had an animal and some lines that could have been letters. Except that the

This drawing shows how the ancient gateway at Harappa would have looked 4,500 years ago. Offices for tax collectors and guards were located along the right side. A wooden bridge would have covered the large drain in the center of the gateway to allow traffic to move into the city.

66 Carved stone seal, Harappa, Pakistan, 2200–2000 BCE

This two-inch (five-centimeter) square unicorn seal belonged to a powerful leader of Harappa. He may have used it to stamp clay seals that were attached to bundles of traded goods.

creature on his seal was not the usual bull or tiger, but something that looked like a one-horned bull—a unicorn. And if the lines were the letters or symbols of a language, it was not a script anyone had ever seen before.

Alexander Cunningham spent the rest of his life thinking that his dig at Harappa in the Punjab had been a failure. He never realized that the seal he had found was a key to an unknown civilization, a civilization that no one ever suspected had existed. Before the seal was found at Harappa, archaeologists had believed that the oldest cities in India and Pakistan dated from about 700 BCE. They were wrong. The crumbling bricks that the engineers had used to raise the railroad out of the mud were 5,000 years old. They were what was left of an ancient civilization as large and well organized as those of Egypt and Mesopotamia. Historians call it the Indus civilization.

The Indus civilization peaked with 1,500 settlements and several large cities, some with populations of up to 80,000 people. Its artisans were among the most skilled in the world, and its people traded with Mesopotamia and Central Asia. But in some ways, it was an easy civilization to overlook. Its people didn't build great pyramids or fancy tombs, as the Egyptians did. They didn't fight great battles and leave a great written legacy, like the Mesopotamians.

Have you ever met someone who looks totally ordinary, but turns out to have a really interesting life? Maybe she plays in a rock band. Or he designs theme park rides. The people of the Indus civilization left no great monuments behind. But that's because they were too busy making a good life for themselves, lives whose richness was in the living, not the stuff they left behind. It wasn't until the early

1920s that archaeologists realized that there might be more in the mounds of crumbling brick than met the eye. And so, 30 years after Sir Alexander Cunningham's death in 1893, archaeologists finally rediscovered the great city of Harappa.

Harappa was built on a low ridge between the Ravi and Satluj Rivers. It was a good location for a city. The land was fertile and villagers could hunt for animals and gather wood for fuel in the nearby forests. The rivers kept the fields around the city well watered, and the mud from floods made the land fertile. Lakes full of fish sparkled in the distance. Traveling merchants liked to stop in Harappa, where they could get a good meal and a snug bed safe behind the mud-brick city walls.

As it happens, Harappa's city walls are as mysterious as its script, the signs and symbols Cunningham found on the stone seal. Building and taking care of town walls must have been expensive and complicated. The earliest city wall at Harappa was 8 feet wide (2.5 meters) and may have stood more than 13 feet (4 meters) high. Archaeologists have added up the work hours required to dig the clay, shape and dry the mud bricks, mix the mortar that joined the bricks together, bring materials to the site by oxcart, and then actually build the wall. They estimate that it would have taken more than 500 people a full three months to construct a city wall when Harappa was still a small city. The city walls must have been very important—but why?

Most cities build walls to keep enemies out. But Harappa didn't seem to have enemies, at least any that were willing to attack it. Archaeologists have not found many weapons or pictures of warfare in Harappa. The city walls show no sign of attack and don't seem to have been designed for defense. If an enemy got past the massive gateway, the orderly streets and open courtyards

More than 150 years ago, local workers removed most of the bricks of the gateway and walls at Harappa to help build the foundation for the nearby railway tracks.

TOO MUCH SALT!

Four hundred miles to the south of Harappa, the city of Mohenjo Daro lies baking under the hot Pakistani sun. Archaeologists began excavating Mohenjo Daro in the 1920s and 1930s, at the same time as Harappa, but they stopped in 1965. The bricks that make up Mohenjo Daro's buildings are crumbling. Minerals and salts from centuries of irrigation water have built up in the soil and soaked into the bricks. As the bricks dry in the hot summer, the salts crystallize and make the bricks crumble. Today archaeologists are trying to figure out the best way to preserve the exposed buildings.

❝ Public well and bathing platforms, Harappa, about 2500 BCE

An ancient well at Mohenjo Daro, made with wedge-shaped bricks, still draws the curious tourists. The upper layers of the walls and buildings have been covered with modern mud bricks to protect the original ancient bricks.

caravan + serai = "group of merchants" + "inn"
Caravanserai comes from Persian.

inside the city would have been hard to defend.

If the city wall wasn't meant to protect against war, maybe it was meant to keep out thieves. But most thieves probably would have preferred to rob travelers or traders when they were alone in the desert or forest. The city walls *did* help protect against another kind of threat—the floodwaters of the nearby Ravi River. But perhaps the most important function of the walls was to help the city collect the taxes needed in order to maintain its walls, clean its streets, and protect its people.

By 2600 BCE, Harappa had two major walled sections, each with gateways that could control who entered the city. Walls also surrounded the suburbs next to these large sections. In one suburb, archaeologists found a massive gateway with several small rooms alongside the entryway. In the litter filling the rooms, they found seals, broken clay impressions or sealings, and stone weights, the ancient world's version of pens, stamps, and weight registers. Those rooms were offices, probably for inspectors who taxed all goods coming into and going out of the city.

When traders arrived at a city, they parked their oxcarts outside the city gates at a place that was part-hotel, part-warehouse called a *caravanserai*. Staying outside the city meant that the merchants could come and go from the caravanserai as they pleased without worrying about the city gates, which were probably only open between morning and evening. They could also leave things locked in their rooms that they didn't intend to sell, so that they wouldn't have to pay taxes on them.

When the merchants entered the city, inspectors stationed at the gates broke open the sealed bundles of trade goods to examine what the merchants had brought to sell. The merchants probably had to pay a tax for the right to sell their goods in the city. After the inspectors had decided how much tax to charge and the merchants had paid, they were free to take their goods to the market. When inspectors broke the clay sealing on a bundle of goods, they would throw it into the street, where it would dissolve with the rains. But sometimes the clay sealing was swept into the trash and burned. Archaeologists later found these hardened sealings.

Customers bought things with grain and finished goods such as stone beads or textiles (cloth), which the merchant could trade somewhere else. When the day's trading was done, the merchant took his pay to the gateway. After the inspectors had examined and weighed the grain and finished goods, they may have sealed each bundle with a small lump of clay stamped with the city official's mark to show

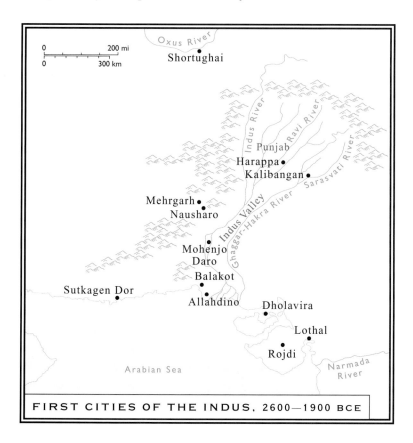

FIRST CITIES OF THE INDUS, 2600—1900 BCE

A modern worker can carry about 7 small bricks weighing a total of 150 pounds on his head. This would be the equivalent of 5 of the 30-pound mud bricks used at ancient Harappa to build the city wall.

that the merchant had paid his exit taxes. Then the merchant could leave.

By 2600 BCE, baked-brick houses filled Harappa and drains removed dirty water from the city. Each walled neighborhood had its own market and craft workshops. Potters and metalsmiths built their workshops at the edges of the settlement, so that the cinders from their furnaces and kilns would not land on nearby houses. Copper craftsmen worked along the southern edge of the city. The winds usually came from the north and would blow the smoke and cinders away from the city.

People built houses with small rooms, some of which were used for storing food. Households opened onto courtyards that served as kitchens and workshops. Some houses had two stories with stairs along one wall. Almost every house had a flat roof that people used for sleeping in the summer and as extra work space.

People put their garbage in large clay pots stuck into the floor in rooms along the edge of the street. Some of these large jars set into the ground may have served as toilets that laborers cleaned out every so often. Most houses also had bathing areas and drains that emptied into pots or larger drains in the street.

The system worked really well, as long as the merchants kept coming and paying the taxes that built the walls and drains and paid the laborers who maintained them. But by about 1900 BCE, after 700 comfortable years, things began to change. For reasons scholars still don't fully understand, fewer traders were willing to risk the dangers of traveling through desert and forest. We know there were fewer traders because archaeologists have found fewer valuable items from distant places. Because fewer traders were paying taxes, the cities could no longer afford to keep up their walls and inspectors. Changes in the course of the Indus River and its tributaries, combined with increased flooding may well have added to Harappa's problems. There may have been other reasons as well. Reasons that can only be found with further excavations. And someday, perhaps we will be able to read the Indus script.

CHAPTER 6

SCRATCHES, SEALS, AND SYMBOLS
THE BIRTH OF WRITING

What do you think is the world's most important invention? The wheel? The light bulb? If you asked most historians, they wouldn't hesitate: reading and writing, all the way. Just as pottery allowed ancient people to store food and goods in a place safe from water or insects, writing let people store knowledge. For the first time, the things people knew could be kept safe for their children, and not lost through their poor memories, sicknesses, or deaths. What's more, writing meant people could pass on information to others in different places or times. As long as people can read, they can know. The ability to read and write was—and is—power.

Like a child who draws pictures before he or she writes words, ancient people first used symbols instead of letters. The first evidence for writing comes from pottery **shards**. Many ancient pots have marks on them that potters probably made before the clay was baked hard. That way each potter could tell which pots were hers, even when she shared a kiln with her neighbors. That's probably the first kind of writing you learned, too—your name, so you could mark every paper and drawing you made as *yours*. People started using these simple markings as early as 4500 BCE in the Indus Valley and continued using them long after the invention of writing.

Potter's marks are scratched into the clay *before* firing, but many finished pieces of pottery have symbols that were scratched into them *after* they were fired, probably by their new owners. No one knows for sure what these symbols stand for. Archaeologists think that they might have been labels that identified the contents of the pot, the name of the owner, or perhaps the name of the person to whom it

{ Shards are pieces of broken pottery.

Pottery shards, Harappa, Pakistan, 3300–2800 BCE

was being sent. If, for example, a wealthy man sent a pot of honey to a temple as an offering, he might have wanted to identify either himself or the temple where he was sending the gift.

Symbols scratched into pots after they were fired are called **graffiti**. Graffiti probably developed at the same time as potter's marks, around 4000 BCE, but the earliest examples from Harappa date to around 3300 BCE. They count as the earliest evidence for writing in the Indus Valley. By about 2800–2600 BCE, the symbols that began as graffiti had become a written language, one that was spreading rapidly throughout the region.

From the Italian word *graffito,* meaning "a scratch." *Graffiti* was first used to describe the words scratched on the painted walls of Pompeii, Italy, a city that was destroyed by a volcano in 79 CE.

Why did writing spread so quickly? For one thing, it was useful, especially to merchants who traveled throughout the Indus Valley. They used square seals with animal designs and bold script across the top to seal goods for trade. They also developed a system of tablets for keeping accounts. Archaeologists have recently found a

⟨⟨ Elephant steatite seal, Mohenjo Daro, Pakistan, 2600–1900 BCE

building that was a kind of "mint" that made the tablets that merchants used to keep track of their goods.

Merchants weren't the only people who were quick

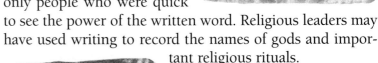

to see the power of the written word. Religious leaders may have used writing to record the names of gods and important religious rituals.

⟨⟨ Glazed tablet, Harappa, Pakistan, 2450–2200 BCE

Archaeologists have been trying to understand the Indus script for more than a hundred years—without any luck. For one thing, they've only found about 2,000 examples of it, and none of the examples has more than 23 symbols (most have only five). But they have been able to figure out a few of its features. They know that the Indus script is not directly related to any known writing system. They know that it was

⟨⟨ Copper tablet, Mohenjo Daro, Pakistan, 2200–1900 BCE

written from right to left (as is the script used to write Urdu, the modern language of Pakistan). But sometimes longer inscriptions are written from the right in the first line, then from left to right on the next line, and so on, back and forth until the end. This type of writing style is called *boustrophedon*, a Greek word that means "as the ox turns," because it moves down one row and up the next, the way oxen plow a field, or people mow the lawn.

Archaeologists know that the Indus script probably used both symbol-pictures and letters standing for different sounds. They have made out between 400 and 450 symbols, which are too few for a language without an alphabet and too many for a language with an alphabet. The script of the Mesopotamians, for example, used more than 600 symbols, each of which stood for a syllable and sometimes also for a whole word. The Canaanites, who lived to the west of Mesopotamia, later developed an alphabet of fewer than 50 symbols, each standing for a specific consonant.

A lot of the examples we have of Indus script come from inscriptions on seals. The square seals of the Indus cities were made from a soft stone called **steatite**, or soapstone. The original color of the stone ranges from gray or tan to white. If the steatite was going to be used for a seal, the seal maker bleached it with a chemical solution and fired it in a kiln to make it hard and white. (For 100 years, archaeologists have been trying to figure out what that solution was, but no luck yet.) Some seals were made from faience paste that could be molded, fired, and glazed. Faience is made from ground quartz that is melted and then reground to make a glassy paste. It can be colored with copper to make a blue-green or turquoise color, and then fired at high temperatures to make a shiny glazed object.

Seals were important symbols of power. Once an ancient South Asian "sealed" a box or a door with a piece of clay he had stamped with his seal, no one could open it without the sealer's permission. People who did not own anything of great value had no need for

"Steatite" is from *steatos* (Greek), meaning "suet," the hard fat from cows and sheep used to make soap. Also called soapstone, steatite is such a soft stone that a little comes off on your hands when you rub it, making it feel soapy. Its powdered form is talcum powder.

Clay impression of seal, Harappa, Pakistan, 2800–2600 BCE

You can still see faint traces of writing and other symbols on this clay seal from the early city levels at Harappa.

INDUS VALLEY WRITING

4500 BCE
Early potter's marks on pottery in Baluchistan and Mehrgarh

3300 BCE
Earliest writing/graffiti on pottery from Harappa, early village culture

2800 BCE
Early Indus script at Harappa, early city culture

2600–1900 BCE
Indus script found at all major Indus cities and towns, full-fledged city culture

seals, so scholars suspect that they were used only by wealthy traders, landowners, or religious leaders. Because seals were so valuable, working like a signature that could be used to approve payments and trade, the city government probably controlled seal making.

Once a seal was made, probably only one person used it. But sometimes a father might pass a seal down to his son, or a mother to her daughter. After a seal had been used for a while, its edges would get worn and rounded. It would no longer make very clear impressions. Since people wouldn't want anyone else using their seal, they were very careful about getting rid of their worn-out seals. Archaeologists at Harappa have uncovered heavily worn seals buried in the floor of a house. Lots of broken seals and tablets have also been discovered in the litter filling the streets or in trash pits. The ancient Indus people either buried their old seals or broke them into small pieces before they threw them away, the same way people today cut up their old credit cards.

But the ancient South Asians have nothing to fear from the archaeologists who found them—at least until someone figures out how to read the script the seals are written in! Until someone finally gets to the bottom of that script, we'll never know the whole story of Harappa and her sister cities. No matter how carefully we look at the puzzle pieces, some of them are still missing. Even so, archaeologists have a lot of fun trying to put them together.

LONG LIVE THE UNICORN!

Two-thirds of the seals found in the Indus Valley include a picture of a unicorn. What this means, nobody is sure, but these are the world's first unicorns. Indus seals with unicorn designs have been found in Mesopotamia. The symbol probably spread from there to the Mediterranean and Europe. It may have spread as far as China, where tradition has it that the gift of writing was given to the Emperor Fu Xi by a unicorn. This 4,500-year-old unicorn was found in Pakistan. A hole in its belly was used to hold it on a stick like a puppet.

CHAPTER 7

TRASH AND TOILETS
THE CITIES OF THE INDUS

Archaeologists can't read the records the people of the Indus Valley left because they haven't decoded the script. So they have to use other clues—like trash. What's left of people's ruined basements, garbage, and sewers tell us a lot about what it was like to live in the Indus Valley 4,000 years ago.

Sometimes ancient cities are buried through tragic events such as an earthquake or a volcanic eruption. But usually cities get buried bit by bit, while people are still living there. Old buildings fall down and are covered with dust and garbage. Because it's easier, people build on top of the old buildings rather than clear them out and start from the ground again. As this happens, the streets are repaved and get higher and higher over time.

The cities of Mohenjo Daro and Harappa, located in what is now Pakistan, had enough room for 40,000 to 80,000 people. That's about as many people as can fit into the huge Olympic stadium in Athens. But no one is sure if that many people actually lived there full-time. How many of those buildings were empty during the farming season, when people may have gone home to their family farms to help with planting and harvesting? How many of the buildings sheltered merchants or pilgrims who were just passing through? Or people who had come to celebrate religious festivals?

The streets of Indus towns and cities in India and Pakistan are strangely similar. Each has streets that run north and south and east and west. Why? No one knows, although religious beliefs might have had something to do with it. For example, Christian cathedrals face the rising sun in the east and Muslims pray facing their sacred city, Mecca.

Although they were made by hand and not machine, the fired bricks used for building in the cities came in just one size and shape: a rectangle about 11 inches long and 5 ½

Narrow side streets at Mohenjo Daro, Pakistan, connect the private neighborhoods with the main streets. High walls keep the streets in cool shadows during the hot summer.

inches wide (28 cm by 14 cm). These fired bricks were so strong that some of them have been recycled and are being reused in modern buildings. Bricks weren't the only things that were the same size—walls and doorways throughout the Indus Valley are about the same size and design. Even wells were lined with the same styles of wedge-shaped bricks. And every city had a drainage system for carrying away rainwater and sewage from toilets and bathing areas.

Who decided to make one-size-fits-all bricks? Who said that streets *had* to run north/south and east/west? Today's cities are full of differences—the size, style, **orientation**, and building materials of any ten buildings are almost never the same. So why were the ancient Indus cities so similar?

Maybe because one person—or one small group of people—was making all the decisions. Maybe a strong government or strong religious leaders told everyone what to do. But there is no sign of large palaces or temples—the buildings of powerful governments and religious leaders. Perhaps the people of the Indus Valley had religious or historical beliefs that taught them that they should build everything in the same way. No one knows for sure.

The cities of the Indus Valley were very well organized. They were divided into walled neighborhoods, with each neighborhood specializing in one kind of work. Potters lived in one area, and coppersmiths lived in another. People probably lived with their extended families—children, parents, cousins, aunts and uncles, and grandparents—all doing the same kind of work.

Say you were a merchant from Oman, in what is now known as the Middle East, come to Harappa to trade alabaster vases and fine woolen cloth for shell bangles and stone beads. The first thing you would have noticed was what *wasn't* there—no great temples or monuments, like the ones you had seen in the cities of Mesopotamia and Persia. You probably would have thought Harappa a poor place, without the grandeur of home. But then you would have noticed the tidy, neat streets. Even as a stranger in a strange city, you didn't have to leave extra time in case you got lost in the maze of streets every time you went to the

"Orient" is from the Latin word *orior*, to rise. The sun rises in the east each day, and when you orient yourself, you are figuring out where you are and which direction you are facing.

market. The streets were straight and predictable, and quieter than you were used to. Houses weren't open to the street, so you didn't hear every word that people were saying inside as you walked by. Instead, the main doorway of each house was located along a side street and had an entryway that screened the inside from curious eyes. The windows opened onto the courtyard at its center.

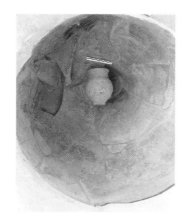

You'd have noticed that the city smelled better than most cities you visited. Major streets had built-in garbage bins. Each block of houses had a private well and bathrooms with drains. The small drains leading from the bathing areas and toilets emptied into slightly larger drains in the side streets that flowed into huge covered sewers in the main streets, big enough for people to climb inside and clean. These big city sewers emptied outside of the city wall into gullies and were washed out every year by the rains.

As you wandered through the city, you would have seen one building that stood out from all the others, the so-called Great Hall. Not only was it bigger than all of the other buildings, but it was also built of wood on a brick foundation. (Because the local trees were small, the builders probably bought the wood in the highlands, then floated it down the rivers to the city during the monsoon.) Archaeologists don't know what the building was used for. At first, they guessed that it was used to store grain, but there's no evidence of that. Today, they believe that Harappa's Great Hall, as well as a similar large building in Mohenjo Daro, was probably a government or public meeting place.

Although the great cities of the Indus were very similar, they were not identical. If you were a pilgrim from Harappa arriving in Mohenjo Daro for a religious festival, you might have felt that the people in Mohenjo Daro were a little bit more formal than your friends at home. For one thing,

GOING TO THE BATHROOM, HARAPPAN STYLE

Some people may have walked outside the city wall to the nearby fields to go to the bathroom, as is commonly done today in much of rural Asia. But many houses had toilets that were separate from the bathing areas. The toilets were large jars called sump pots sunk into the floor, and many of them contained a small jar of water for washing after using the toilet. Sometimes these sump pots were connected to a drain to let sewage flow out, and most had a tiny hole at the bottom to let water seep into the ground. To keep the whole thing smelling better, people occasionally scattered clean sand in the bathroom and toilet.

Mohenjo Daro didn't have just a Great Hall, but many other large buildings as well. Each section of the city had several large complexes. Some of these buildings may have been religious buildings or mansions for wealthy merchants. One building had a circle of bricks in its courtyard, which might have been the site of a sacred tree. A double staircase led to an upper courtyard surrounded by several rooms. When archaeologists excavated it, they found that the house was littered with lots of seals and fragments of a stone sculpture depicting a seated man wearing a cloak over his left shoulder who might have been a political or religious leader of some kind.

Stone head, Mohenjo Daro, Pakistan, 2200–2000 BCE

This stone head is a part of a larger seated statue. The braided hair is bound with a headband, and a hole in the top of the head may have held an elaborate headdress.

But as a pilgrim, you would probably have been most interested in the large building that today is called the Great Bath. You would go first into a small bathing area that was supplied with a well. You'd take off your outer clothes, which were dusty from your journey, and wash yourself. Once you were clean, you would move on into a large courtyard. You might walk along the roofed edges of the courtyard to better admire the sacred pool in the center. When you were ready for the bath that would clean your spirit as well as your body, you would walk into the large pool by one of the two wide stairways that led down into the healing water.

Travelers from both Mohenjo Daro and Harappa probably would have felt least at home in Dholavira, the third major city of the Indus. Dholavira, located in what is now the modern country of India, was on an island in an inland bay far to the south of Mohenjo Daro. The farming was not good in the areas around Dholavira—the climate was too dry—so most people supported themselves by herding, fishing, and trading. To collect and store enough rainwater, the people of Dholavira built stone tanks or reservoirs that stretched over more than a third of their city.

Dry Dholavira may not have had much mud, but it had lots of stone. Most of its houses and drains were made of sandstone blocks. Dholavira was the grandest of the cities, with huge walls and ceremonial gates separating the quarters of the city. One of the gates was even topped by an inscription of ten symbols, each one a little more than a foot tall.

❝ Great Bath, Mohenjo Daro, Pakistan, about 2000 BCE

The Great Bath at Mohenjo Daro, the only one of its kind, was used for public ceremonies and bathing rituals.

Dholavira's magnificent gates couldn't change the fact that, in general, the people of the Indus Valley cities did not choose to build huge monuments to a king or religious ruler. Their cities were simple and workaday, without unnecessary flourishes or great pieces of monumental art. But towering high above the plain, with gleaming red-brick gateways and light gray mud-brick walls, they still must have been a commanding sight.

MY LIFE AS A HOUSE

The orientation of a house and the placement of its rooms is based on the sacred "foundation man," or *Vastu Purusha*. When drawn as a square, the head is located in the northeast corner. This was supposed to be the most fortunate part of the house. The kitchen goes here. The southwest corner, where the feet are located is thought to be facing the direction of Yama, the god of death. There are no doors on this side, so that the evil spirits from the land of death can't enter the house.

ARCHAEOLOGIST AT WORK:
AN INTERVIEW WITH
HEATHER M.-L. MILLER

Heather M.-L. Miller is an assistant professor of anthropology at the University of Toronto. She specializes in Harappan pyrotechnics, processes that use fire to change materials, such as turning clay into pottery, ore into copper, and sand into faience. She is also interested in medieval trade routes between South Asia and Central Asia.

When did you begin to go on digs?
While I was in college. But I started late. Some of my colleagues started when they were kids by going to day programs where you'd volunteer for a day and do some digging.

Did you decide to go to South Asia because that's where your professors were working?
No. Not at all. I had to work really hard to get over there. I knew I wanted to work on ancient cities, but there are lots of places where I could do that. I'm from southern California, kind of the edge of the desert, and it's what I was used to, so I wanted to work some place arid, where you aren't tortured to death by bugs. I also wanted to go somewhere the snakes stay on the ground instead of dropping on you. My undergraduate professors at Rice University worked in West Africa, where there is completely fascinating archaeology, but way too many diseases.

What did you do at Harappa?
I looked for kiln sites, to see where in the city people were manufacturing pottery, copper, faience, and other things. I did what's

called a total walkover. That means I walked over the entire surface of the site at one-meter intervals with a very good assistant looking for a special type of debris characteristic of these crafts. You get melted bits of pottery, or pieces of crucible [small pots used for melting metal] with a little bit of metal left on it. We found that they were manufacturing in lots of different parts of the city. There wasn't a special quarter, like an industrial park.

Was there anything especially interesting in the debris?
One thing was kind of cool. They melted their metal in clay containers called crucibles. But this clay melts at a lower temperature than metal, so they figured out how to temper the clay by adding straw. The straw insulated the clay so that it didn't melt. Adding straw also reduced the cracking that happens when you fire pots. The straw burns away, and there's room for the clay to expand where the straw used to be, so it doesn't crack. We also found some little dish things with powdered steatite on it. We

think they used it kind of like Teflon. Steatite doesn't melt at these temperatures, so whatever was on it would slip off instead of melting together with clay.

What do you like best about being an archaeologist?
I like the combination of physical work and mental work and plain old accounting. I like that sometimes you're inside, sometimes you're outside. Sometimes you're being very scientific. Sometimes you're just standing there, shoveling dirt. But mostly it's solving puzzles. We all like working out puzzles. I've noticed that a lot of archaeologists like murder mysteries. It's all about curiosity. That's the real draw—you're curious about people that lived before.

What do you not like about it?
I've managed to avoid all the things I was sure I wouldn't like, like working in swamps and stuff. It's not easy for me to write, but writing is a very important part of what I do, so I'm constantly trying to be a better writer.

What has surprised you the most about being an archaeologist?
What I had to get accustomed to is that you never find out the answer, because there are always more questions. And if you don't like surprises, you won't like being an archaeologist. It's one surprise after another.

Do you feel that you get to know the people who lived in the places you are excavating?
You really do. For one thing, there are fingerprints all over everything. You know, they're patting the clay and then it gets fired. And even though Harappa is a pretty dis-

turbed site, every once in a while you stumble on something that is obviously just the way someone left it. We were digging in this little alley behind a house and found a little pit someone had dug, with some river mussels in it. It was their leftover lunch. And the Harappans are very creative people. Their figurines have a lot of character. It's hard to see humor across the centuries, but I certainly see people having a lot of fun with those figurines. Or maybe having a connection would be a better way to say it, since some of them are scary. Plus, my colleague is very good at that sort of thing. We'll find a pendant and he'll say someone must have been really upset to lose that.

If you could have one question answered about the sites you've excavated, what would it be?
I think I would probably want to know how the five great cities of the Indus were connected. Were they independent? Did the same family rule them all? That's what I'd like to know.

I think the really important thing about archaeology is that it connects people with the past. It's something we all share. No one in my family came from South Asia, but now I feel like that's a part of my heritage, too. Knowing about how those people solved their problems of living together in cities makes me think about the ways we try to solve a lot of the same problems in our cities today. The Indus people were so creative. I feel a lot of respect for them. And I feel like I share something with my colleagues in Pakistan. I think people need to appreciate each other's history.

CHAPTER 8

GOING SHOPPING
ARTS AND CRAFTS
IN THE INDUS VALLEY

During the holidays, big cities like New York and London are even more crowded than usual. Why do people go to all the trouble and expense to travel to a big city? Because the stores are better. And because big cities are fun. They have theaters and museums and major-league sports. And even more activities than usual are going on during the holidays, like Thanksgiving and New Year's Day parades and holiday concerts and performances.

The weeks after the spring and fall harvests were probably a holiday for the people of the Indus Valley civilization. Farmers, fishermen, and herders gathered their goods and their families and made the long trip to the nearest city to sell their goods and thank the gods for the bounty of the harvest. Imagine the son of a farmer who is 12 or 13—old enough to bear the two-day walk to Harappa one autumn in about 2100 BCE. We'll call this boy Sarang. Sarang would have

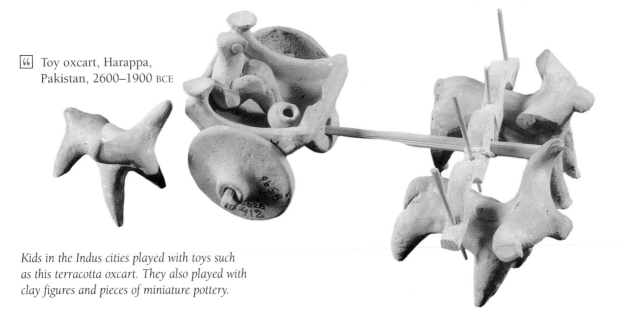

66 Toy oxcart, Harappa,
Pakistan, 2600–1900 BCE

Kids in the Indus cities played with toys such as this terracotta oxcart. They also played with clay figures and pieces of miniature pottery.

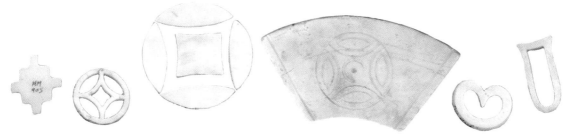

begun the journey by helping to load the family's oxcart with the barley, wheat, and cotton that they had raised that year on their farm. He may have helped to harness the oxen that pulled the heavy load. He was probably wildly excited—and probably driven crazy by the oxen's slow pace through the wooded countryside and by the loud creaking of the cart.

If they lived too far away to make the journey in a single day, Sarang and his family would have set up camp with other travelers they had met along the way to help protect their goods from the bandits who hid in the forest. Eventually they would have emerged from the forest to see the walled city of Harappa in the distance, rising pale and beautiful above the plain.

If they arrived in the evening or early morning, they could have seen the fires of the coppersmiths and potters along the southern edge of the city. The wind blows from the north in Harappa. Limiting furnaces to the southern side of the city meant that their sparks would be blown away from the crowded city streets. As Sarang got closer to the city, he would have realized that the wind carried more than sparks. The leather dressers also worked on the edge of the city, and the stink of dead animals, which in some poor neighborhoods were left to rot on the street, must have been awful.

Once inside the city gates, the sights and sounds of the crowded market would most likely have overwhelmed a farm boy like Sarang. One part of the city specialized in wood carving and carpentry. Here his mother could have bought cedar chests to keep the family's clothing safe from moths and insects. Stonecutters, who made everything from drills to grinding stones to sharp stone blades, lived in

This white conch shell inlay, found in a workshop at Mohenjo Daro, could have been put into jewelry or furniture for decoration or religious symbolism.

another quarter. Sarang would have seen booths selling carved ivory ornaments, polished until they were smooth as butter, and **inlay** for wooden furniture.

Jewelers clustered at the center of the market, their workbenches glittering with gold and silver pendants inlaid with precious stones. Strings of beads carved from hard stones of every color hung in the stalls of bead makers. Sarang's family may have bought beads here, but they probably could not have afforded a belt of carnelian beads. Archaeologists estimate that, given the hardness of the drill bits available to the people of Harappa, bead makers would need more than three days to drill a hole in a bead three and one-half inches long. Some of the carnelian beads found on belts are almost twice as long. From start to finish, including all the stages of making a belt, it would have taken one worker more than 480 working days to complete a belt of 36 beads. No wonder archaelogists have found only three carnelian belts.

❝ Carnelian belt, Mohenjo Daro, Pakistan, 2200–2000 BCE

The long, narrow carnelian beads of this elegant belt make a delicate clinking sound when it's worn around the waist. It would have been worn by a very wealthy and powerful woman.

Other shops specialized in the ceramic art of faience, their shelves stocked with beads and bangles as well as small bottles for perfume and medicines. Still others offered white soapstone beads and pendants, delicately fashioned inlay, and intricately carved and inscribed seals with geometric designs. At this same shop, merchants could have ordered inscribed seals with special animal designs that stood for their clan or religious beliefs.

Seals show a person who talks to tigers from a thorny tree. Other seals and figurines show mother goddesses; a bearded, horned god; or the ritual killing of a water buffalo.

This seal shows a god or goddess with three faces wearing bangles on both arms and a headdress made with horns and a branch. The figure sits on his or her heels, in yogic position, on a throne with feet in the shape of animal hooves.

Many of these scenes include a holy man sitting on his heels and meditating in the shade of the pipal, or sacred fig, tree. Archaeologists believe that communities of holy men practiced the discipline of **yoga** in sacred groves outside the city walls. Sarang's family may well have gone to visit these holy men to bring them offerings as part of the harvest festival.

Sarang's family certainly would have stopped in the potter's quarter to buy pots and small clay figurines for worship at the harvest festival. If Sarang had glanced into the courtyard behind any potter's shop, he might well have seen children at work. Artisans' shops were attached to their homes and workshops, and their children would have helped with simple tasks, such as sweeping or fetching materials. Archaeologists have found that some of the flat clay disks that were used to cover pots have child-sized hand- and footprints pressed into

Yoga = "union" in Sanskrit, or union with the Supreme Spirit. Yoga is a series of exercises designed to help people learn to concentrate. At first, people used it focus their attention on religious worship. Today, many people practice yoga to relax.

This stone sculpture from Mohenjo Daro, Pakistan, shows a bearded man seated with one knee raised and one knee tucked underneath him. One eye has a piece of shell inlay still in place.

WHO ARE THE HINDUS?

Most people living in India today worship gods such as Krishna and the goddess Devi and make fire sacrifices. The beliefs and practices are grouped together under the general term Hinduism. This religious tradition has roots extending back into the Indus period around 2600–1900 BCE, where certain symbols, such as the swastika, which represents good luck and the pipal leaf design, which stands for fertility, were first used. Like most religious practices, Hindu ways of worship changed over time.

them. Bead makers' children, with their small hands and good eyesight, probably also helped string tiny beads.

Besides pots, potters made small figurines that were used as offerings to the gods. Even today, many Hindus use small clay or paper figures as part of their prayers and offerings to the gods. Could some of the gods and goddesses they worship have come from Harappan times? No one knows.

Harappan cities were orderly, well-organized places—were they possibly controlled by kings? One clue led some early scholars to think that they might have been. The most famous stone sculpture of the Indus valley is called the Priest King. It's one of only nine stone sculptures, mostly of men, that have been found at Mohenjo Daro. All were broken and defaced, which probably means that the people they represented had lost favor. The lower half of the Priest King is missing, but most stone sculptures with a preserved, lower portion are seated with one knee bent to the

[66] Priest King, Mohenjo Daro, Pakistan, about 2000 BCE

This broken Priest-King sculpture from about 4,000 years ago wears a patterned cloak that was originally colored red and blue or green. It may depict an important clan leader from Mohenjo Daro.

On this seal, a kneeling bearded figure wearing a horned headdress worships a tree god. A worshipper has placed an offering of a person's head on a small stool. A horned mythical ram and seven worshippers complete the scene.

ground and the other raised. People sitting in this position are seen on many of the Indus seals worshipping a deity in a tree or a figure seated in a cross-legged yoga position. This suggests that the sculpture does not represent a priest-king, as its name suggests, but instead an important clan or community leader.

We know a lot about the objects Sarang and his family would have seen in the town, but many questions remain. What was the harvest festival like? Would Sarang and his family have seen dancing and heard singing? Were there plays about the gods? Or were the celebrations solemn, with fasting and prayer? We can only guess. But it's probably safe to say that Sarang would have thought that his trip to the city was one of the most exciting times of the year.

YOU CAN'T TAKE IT WITH YOU

In both Egypt and Mesopotamia, wealthy people and royalty were buried with many of their most valuable possessions. In the Indus Valley, however, women were buried with just a few ornaments, such as shell bangles and sometimes a copper ring or a mirror or small amulet. In South Asia today, glass wedding bangles and personal good luck charms are seldom passed on to another person, but are broken, burned or buried with the dead. The ornaments included with Harappan burials were probably just such special objects that could not be passed on to the next generation. But most valuable items, such as seals, metal tools, and everyday jewelry were kept for living people to use.

" MESOPOTAMIAN
JEWELRY AND
INSCRIPTION, TABLET
AND RIVERBOAT
MODEL IN PAKISTAN,
AND VALMIKI

BY LAND AND BY SEA
TRADE WITH THE NEAR EAST

Have you ever learned a new word, a word you are sure you have never seen before? But after you learn it, this brand-new word suddenly pops up everywhere—in English and history books, on TV, on the radio, and on billboards, until you feel as though it is following you around? The discovery of the Indus Valley civilizations in the 1920s worked a little bit like that, too. Archaeologists looking at sites that dated around 2000 BCE everywhere from Mesopotamia to Oman to Central Asia began noticing little clues left here and there by members of the previously unknown Indus Valley civilization.

In Mesopotamia, for example, archaeologists dug up the tomb of Queen Puabi of Ur. Unlike the practical Harappans, who buried their dead with a few meaningful ornaments and some pottery but kept most of their things for the living to use, Mesopotamian burials were extravagant. In the case of Queen Puabi, for example, more than 20 servants, including armed guards and musicians, went with her into her grave. Her clothing and jewelry and those of her attendants were decorated with copper, carnelian, and lapis lazuli beads and shell inlay—even though Mesopotamia did not have copper mines or sources for the precious stones and shell. She was also buried with a sled and other wooden

" Puabi's jewelry,
Mesopotamia, about
2500 BCE

Queen Puabi's gold necklace is made from lapis lazuli from Afghanistan and carnelian beads from the Indus Valley.

furniture—even though Mesopotamia did not have large trees for lumber. So where on earth did the copper, beads, wood, and shell inlay come from?

This inscription on a tablet was the first clue. According to the records the Mesopotamians kept, these goods came from a land called Meluhha. The great Mesopotamian king Sargon boasted that traders from all over came to his city, called Agade:

> The ships from Meluhha,
> the ships from Magan,
> The ships from Dilmun
> He made tie-up
>   alongside
> The quay of Agade.

At first, no modern scholar knew where Meluhha was. Then archaeologists realized that "Meluhha" must be the Akkadian (a Mesopotamian language) word for the land we know as the Indus Valley. Harappan merchants must have brought the precious stones and beautiful dark wood to Mesopotamia. These merchants would do almost anything for a profit, including sailing to Mesopotamia on the last winds of the winter monsoon.

Imagine a sea captain from Dholavira, on India's northeastern coast, making the last preparations for his annual winter voyage to Mesopotamia. The northeast winds of the retreating monsoon were picking up, and he was anxious to roll the last big pottery storage jars into the hold of his ship. Although no boats from this period have survived, we know from seals and clay models that

66 Sargon, Akkadian tablet, 2250 BCE

This bronze head, possibly of Sargon or his grandson, was made of metal and shell from distant regions, such as the Persian Gulf and the Indus Valley.

" Tablet, Mohenjo Daro, Pakistan, 2200–2000 BCE

This molded terracotta tablet shows a flat-bottomed Indus boat with central cabin. Branches tied to the roof may have been used for protection from bad luck, and travelers took a pet bird along to help guide them to land.

his boat was probably made of wood and included a mast, sail, and central cabin. Shallow-bottomed riverboats, which did not have masts or sails, were also made of wood or of reeds waterproofed with tar—in fact, some bits of tar with the impression of reeds still survive in Oman.

Our captain's crew set up a small kitchen with a cooking area in a corner of the boat protected from the wind. They hung strings of onions and garlic from the roof, and stowed small clay pots filled with ginger, salt, and spices on shelves built along the kitchen's back wall. They piled stacks of firewood and dried cow dung chips for cooking fuel on the deck, wherever they could find room in between long black beams of *shisham* wood (Indian rosewood) for which the Mesopotamian carpenters and shipbuilders would pay a high price.

The crew filled some of the big storage jars with fresh water for the long trip, and packed the others with dried cheese, butter, honey, and beer. They stowed large sacks of wheat and barley toward the front end of the boat, where the sacks were less likely to get wet. Next to the grain, they stacked bales of cotton cloth, bleached white or dyed red or blue. The captain would have bought the cloth from traders who had floated down the shallow rivers that led to the center of the country on their flat-bottomed boats.

" Clay model of a flat-bottomed riverboat, Harappa, Pakistan, 2600–1900 BCE

As you might have guessed from Puabi's tomb, the boat's most valuable cargo was long carnelian beads. These beads were in great demand in Mesopotamia, and the captain wrapped them in soft cotton and packed them carefully in a basket so that they would not get broken during the trip.

After he tied some branches from the sacred pipal tree to the mast to ward off evil spirits, the captain would have loaded his passengers: monkeys, peacocks, and sleek reddish brown hunting dogs to sell as pets, as well as a couple of traders who wanted passage to Mesopotamia.

From Dholavira the captain sailed west across the delta, or the mouth, of the Indus River. With the delta behind him, he faced one of the most dangerous parts of his trip. The coast became very rocky and the crew had to watch for submerged islands as they sailed slowly through waters filled with fish and black-and-gold sea snakes. Once he had made it through that dangerous stretch, the captain could have sailed across the Arabian Sea for a quick stop along the coast of Oman, or chosen to sail directly to Mesopotamia, north through the Persian Gulf. Oman would have been a tempting side trip. The people there were willing to trade their copper, seashells, and pearls, all of which were in high demand in Mesopotamia, for the captain's wood and cotton cloth—but the first traders to arrive in Mesopotamia could charge the highest prices for their goods.

After about a month of travel, the ship from Dholavira arrived at the delta of the Tigris and the Euphrates Rivers. Here they paused until the captain could hire a local fisherman to help guide the ship through the treacherous channels of the delta before it arrived at last in the great city of Ur.

Many people of the Indus Valley had made the trip before, and some of them had probably settled there to live. The captain most likely would have contacted a merchant originally from the Indus Valley to help him convert Mesopotamian weights and measures and interpret for his Akkadian-speaking customers.

The people of southern Mesopotamia may have paid for some of their goods with fine embroidered woolen shawls and blankets. They might also have traded in silver from

Storage jars with narrow bases and painted with black slip like this one (below)—from Harappa around 2400 BCE—could hold 22 gallons of oil. When the jars are filled with oil or grain, they could be easily moved by tipping and rolling them. Ancient traders may have rolled these jars up ramps into waiting oxcarts or boats.

Anatolia, which was widely used in Mesopotamia, and perhaps even in the more valuable gold bangles from Egypt. These simple, round bracelets were a convenient way to measure and carry gold, and could be melted down and made into other objects.

On the slower return journey, the captain stopped at Dilmun, the island that today is called Bahrain, and traded Mesopotamian silver and textiles for pearls from the Persian Gulf. He also stopped at Magan, in what is now Oman, for copper and large, heavy seashells.

Finally, around the beginning of June, the captain would have seen the long red flag at the top of his mast begin to flap in the southwesterly winds. That meant it was time to set sail and catch the winds before the monsoon became too strong. After filling the water pots, he and his crew headed east to the mouth of the Indus and the Gulf of Kutch. The whole trip took almost five months, but he was coming home with a ship full of valuable things that he could sell for a good profit in Dholavira and up the Indus River at Mohenjo Daro.

But the sea captain's voyage proves that the people of the Indus Valley could have been the source of *some* of the goods the Mesopotamians bought from "Meluhha." What about blue lapis lazuli and tin (which they mixed with copper to make bronze), which are not found along either the Indus River or the coast of the Arabian Sea?

It turns out that Indus River merchants followed more than one trade route. According to the later *Ramayana*, an Indian poem by Valmiki, "With the end of the rainy season, nature's traffic resumed on land, air, and water." At the end of October, after the rains were over and the rivers had gone down to their normal levels, a second group of Indus merchants packed their goods into flat-bottomed riverboats and headed north. Their journey upriver was frustratingly slow at first, as men and oxen walking along the banks strained to pull the riverboats against the current. Some ancient clay models of flat-bottomed riverboats have a hole in the center. This hole would have been used for either a mast or a

Valmiki, *Ramayana*, 300–200 BCE

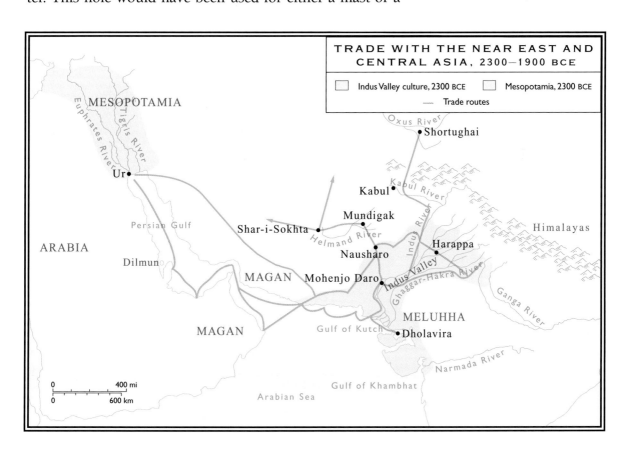

TRADE WITH THE NEAR EAST AND CENTRAL ASIA, 2300–1900 BCE

Indus Valley culture, 2300 BCE   Mesopotamia, 2300 BCE
—— Trade routes

pulling pole. A pulling pole is made by setting up a long pole with a rope tied to the top so that it does not get caught on bushes and trees along the edge of the river. People walk along the river edge pulling the boat, a painfully slow and difficult process that is called "walking" a boat up the river.

The boats would have been even harder to pull laden with grain, butter, oil, and dried fish. Their cargo also included lightweight luxuries such as finely woven cotton, shell bangles, carved ivory gaming pieces for board games, strands of blue-green glazed faience beads, and the exquisite long carnelian beads. Inlaid furniture and painted pottery were packed carefully into woven baskets so that they could be loaded onto pack oxen or carried by porters.

Flat-bottomed ferry boats and oxcarts are still commonly used to transport goods along the Indus River near Mohenjo Daro. The flat bottoms of the boats allow them to move easily along shallow river beds.

The river passage ended at the dangerous deep, narrow passages of the Kabul River, where the merchants left their boats and loaded their goods onto small, hardy mountain cattle and human porters. The trip across the plain near modern Kabul was easier, but once they got to the narrow valleys and high mountain passes of northern Afghanistan, they had to go by foot, leading the pack animals.

They arrived at a small settlement of Indus people in the high valleys of Badakshan sometime in November. These Indus colonists mined lapis lazuli and panned for gold and tin in the river's sands, but they also kept herds of sheep, goat, and cattle, and farmed enough land to provide them with food for most of the year. But they liked being able to buy things from home, and they also wanted grain to trade with nomadic mountain people who brought them more precious stones and metals.

Although they didn't have to find their way through schools of sea snakes and storms at sea, the merchants who traded in the high mountains faced other dangers. Early snows sometimes blocked the high mountain passes, and the monsoon and earthquakes washed the roads away all the time, forcing the merchants to blaze their own paths. So as soon as their trading was done, the merchants of "Meluhha" turned around and headed back down the mountains, eager to get home to snug houses and good friends before the cold days of winter set in.

CHAPTER 10

RIG VEDA, GLASS AND FAIENCE BEADS, AND POTTERY KILN IN PAKISTAN, AND CAVE PAINTING IN INDIA

MYSTERY IN THE CITY
DECLINE AND CHANGE IN THE LATE HARAPPAN PERIOD

Rig Veda, 1700 BCE

"Like a bronze city, surpassing all other rivers and waters, pure in her course from the mountains to the sea" is how the Saraswati River is described in ancient South Asian scripture called the *Rig Veda*. And yet 100 years ago, historians didn't know anything about the river. That's because in about 1900 BCE, the Saraswati River was beginning to dry up. What was a farmer to do? During the Late Harappan period, from 1900 to 1,000 BCE, many people, confused and frightened by the change in the land they knew so well and desperate for food and water, packed up what was left of their shriveled farms and moved to the cities on the Indus and Ravi Rivers or new farmlands in the Ganga plain.

Soon the countryside was no longer good for farmers because the rivers had dried up. Even more people poured into the cities, which were full to overflowing. Looking for safety and shelter, the new immigrants built shacks anywhere they could find a corner to call their own. When the corners were gone, they started building shacks in the middle of the street. The government could not keep up with the overcrowding, and garbage began to build up in the streets.

At about the same time, just after 1900 BCE, merchants stopped traveling to distant places to find precious goods such as turquoise, lapis lazuli, and carnelian to bring to the city to sell. Craftsmen began making glassy faience that *looked* like turquoise, lapis lazuli, and red carnelian for customers who could no longer find the real thing. These look-alikes were so good that they sometimes fooled even modern archaeologists until the "stones" were examined under a microscope. In time the craftsmen learned how to make

Red glass and blue faience beads, Harappa, Pakistan, 1700 BCE true glass that could be colored the reddish brown of carnelian and the black and white of agates, the stone that marbles are made from.

Jewelers weren't the only Late Harappan craftsmen who changed their ways. Potters developed a new kind of kiln that could get hotter faster. This kiln had a hollow center. Holes around the edge of the kiln floor let the fire into the chamber with the pottery. The higher temperatures made pots stronger. So did a new way of working the clay—craftsmen used a wooden paddle and a small lump of clay like an anvil to beat the clay walls of a pot and make the walls thinner and stronger. Working this way, potters could make pots with a rounded base instead of a flat base, which made them easier to balance on the hip or head and easier to pour from. The hot temperatures of the new kilns also let potters try out new kinds of black and red glazes and, in time, different designs. Did a clever, inventive potter bring about these changes? Or did new people moving to the city introduce them?

Potters also began to make small figures of horses, donkeys, and two-humped camels—animals that until this period been used only high in the mountains of Central Asia. What's more, the people using these animals did not write Indus script, although they did use circular seals with geometric designs similar to those found on seals during the Harappan period.

Over time, the new leaders who came to power kept neither written records nor made Harappan-style seals to stamp clay and seal trade goods. This may have been because the trade networks had collapsed, so there was no need for the records. Or it's possible that the new leaders decided not to write down their records.

The way that people buried their dead changed during the Late Harappan times. At first, they changed only the way they placed the bodies, which were buried on their side and oriented northeast to southwest instead of north and

" Kiln, Harappa, Pakistan, 1900–1700 BCE

SONGS AND SACRIFICES

The *Rig Veda* is a collection of Sanskrit chants and hymns sung to gods and goddesses. These gods are a lot like the gods mentioned in stories in Iran and ancient Greece (the Sanskrit father god Indra, for example, is a god of thunder just like the Greek father god Zeus). One of the most important of the *Rig Veda*'s gods was Agni, god of fire, who consumed the food and other gifts worshippers offered to the gods. Archaeologists have found triangular and square-shaped bricks that they believe priests used to make the fire altars to burn sacrifices.

south. The dead were buried with pottery and occasionally ornaments. Later, burial practices *really* changed. The dead body was left in the open and exposed to animals and insects until only the bones were left. Later, people collected the bones of the dead and put them into a large painted jar that was buried along with smaller pots and offerings. The pottery from the earlier burials looked like Harappan pottery—now the urns used for pot burials had very different painted designs. Changing religious ideas during a difficult time could have been the cause of these new styles. Or, a new people might have introduced them.

By 1200 BCE, weapons and tools made of iron began to appear. By 600 BCE, iron was common. Although scholars used to think the South Asians learned how to make iron from people in Turkey, they now believe South Asians discovered it for themselves.

Indra, the Indo-Aryan god of rain and war, carries a sword and a knife in this cave painting in Ajanta, India from 580 CE.

And does the appearance of iron weapons mean that people were fighting wars in South Asia? Scriptures called the *Rig Veda*, which probably come from this time although they weren't written down until several hundred years later, describe forests being cut down as well as the rain and thunder god Indra destroying forts and conquering his enemies:

> With all-outstripping chariot-wheel, O Indra, thou far-famed, hast overthrown the twice ten kings
>   of men...
> Thou goest on from fight to fight **intrepidly**, destroying castle after castle here with strength.

Rig Veda, 1700 BCE

{ People behave intrepidly when they are brave or without fear.

After the discovery of some unburied skeletons on the highest, and therefore latest, street levels at Mohenjo Daro, some scholars assumed that the forts that Indra was destroying were the walled cities of the Indus Valley. But the Late Harappan cities were never destroyed by warfare, and there is no evidence of large groups of people coming from outside South Asia. Historians believe that the mysterious skeletons were people who died from contagious diseases. They were left unburied in abandoned parts of the city so they would not infect the grave diggers.

These unburied skeletons were dumped in an abandoned house in Mohenjo Daro. They were probably victims of an epidemic and not killed in a massacre, as thought by some early archaeologists.

So what happened around 1900 BCE? For many years, historians believed that invaders called **Aryans** poured into the Indus Valley and, with the help of the horse and bronze or iron weapons, destroyed the Late Harappan civilization.

But archaeologists can't find evidence of major warfare, and the body types of the people living in the Indus Valley did not change during this time period. More likely, the disappearing Saraswati River strained the Late Harappan way of life past the breaking point. Satellite photos of the dried riverbed and excavations along its banks show that the river was huge at one time, almost five miles across. As old ways

{ *arya* = "noble ones" in Sanskrit, an ancient language of South Asia. Anyone who spoke Sanskrit and worshipped the gods of the *Rig Veda* was *arya*, or noble.

Indo-Aryan is a name for a family of languages that includes Sanskrit and most languages of northern India and Pakistan. A person who spoke the ancient Sanskrit language was called Arya.

📖 Cave painting, Bhimbetka, India, 1000–800 BCE

In this cave painting the warriors on horseback fighting people on foot may represent the conflicts between Indo-Aryan communities as they moved east and south into the center of the subcontinent.

The Ghaggar-Hakra and Saraswati Rivers began drying up around 1900 BCE. As people left their towns and farmlands for greener pastures, the economy and trade of the Harappan cities began to decline.

of living and trade broke down, the people of the Indus Valley began to look around for other ways to stay alive. People from the countryside and highlands who spoke the **Indo-Aryan** language, people who had known and traded with the Harappans for many years, became more powerful over time until they could challenge the Harappans' power.

Between about 1500 and 600 BCE, Indo-Aryan speakers gained power and conquered areas in the Ganga River valley beyond the lands that the Harappans once controlled. Cave paintings from Central India show them overwhelming the local people with their horses, chariots, and iron weapons. The language and traditions of the Indo-Aryan speakers replaced the old ways of the Harappans, until the Harappans and everything they made—the shining cities, the bustling trade networks, even their language—was lost or buried, forgotten for thousands of years.

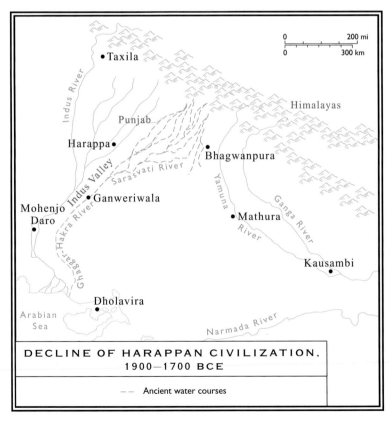

DECLINE OF HARAPPAN CIVILIZATION, 1900–1700 BCE

- - - Ancient water courses

CHAPTER 11

FIRE AND SACRIFICE
LIVING BY THE VEDAS

Imagine you could watch the history of the world as a super-fast movie shot from outer space. If you were watching the South Asian subcontinent, things would look about the same from about 3000 to 2000 BCE with cities, villages, and crops sprinkled throughout the Indus Valley. But about 2000 BCE, the scene would start to change dramatically. Some of the old settlements along what used to be the Saraswati River would disappear as the once-great river dried up. Then you would see spaces opening up in the jungles along the Yamuna and Ganga River valley as new communities moved in. These communities cut down and burned trees to make room for towns, cities, and fields of summer crops watered by the monsoon, such as rice and millet.

We know a lot more about these new communities than we do about the Harappans because we have their scriptures, called the **Vedas**. The Vedas are a collection of hymns, stories, and religious instructions in the Sanskrit language. Sanskrit was not written down at first, and the Vedas were only passed on through memorization. How much can you memorize? Could you memorize a poem? A story? How about a whole book? How about memorizing a whole book by repeating back what your teacher tells you, without having words to look at? How about a whole lot of books?

The Vedas were so important that students spent 10, 15, or even 20 years studying and memorizing them so that they would not be lost from generation to generation. Young boys who belonged to a class of people called Brahmin had to learn the alphabet of the sacred language of Sanskrit before they could begin to learn the hundreds of sacred texts in the Vedas.

One of the hundreds of stories in the Vedas tells us about a 12-year-old boy named Ketu who was getting ready to study the Vedas. On a typical day, Ketu awoke to the

{ The word *Veda* comes from the Sanskrit *vid*, which means "to know." The Vedas are sacred knowledge.

COULD I BORROW YOUR LANGUAGE?

Sanskrit is in the same family as other West Asian and European languages—the Indo-European language family. For example, the Sanskrit word for father is *pitr,* the Latin word is *pater,* and the Spanish is *padre.* Scholars still don't agree about where this large language family started or how it spread over such a vast area. But many words (even the names of gods and goddesses) are so alike that there must have been some contact, maybe through trade, between the communities living in the Indus Valley, Central Asia, Iran, and even Greece.

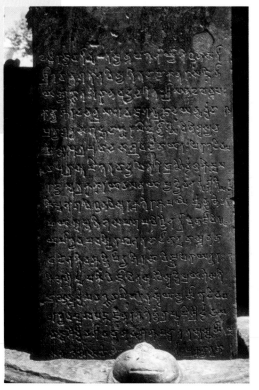

This Sanskrit edict, written in a script called Devanagari, proclaims the conquest of Nepal by King Manavadeva I in 464 CE.

sounds of his mother getting breakfast ready and his older sister sweeping the kitchen in preparation for the morning rituals. The kitchen would have been located in an open courtyard in the northeastern part of the house, the purest and most holy part of the home. The sun hit this area first, warming the mud-plastered walls and bringing light to the courtyard. On cold mornings, Ketu might well have wished that he had been born a girl. His sister got to stay at home and help their mother in the warm kitchen, but he had to bathe in the ice-cold river in the fog before his morning worship of the sun god Surya.

One of the first things Ketu learned as a child was that there were four different *varna,* or classes of people. The Vedas taught that the four *varna* came from the body of Purusha, the cosmic being whose sacrifice resulted in the creation of the universe. The Brahmins, the class of priests, came from the head of Purusha. The Kshatriyas, the warriors and kings, came from his arms, while the Vaisyas, or merchants, came from his thighs, and the Shudras, or peasants, from his feet.

The Vedic peoples believed that people were born into the *varna* they deserved. If a people lived good lives, they would be reborn into a higher class. If they did not live a good life, they came back in a lower class. When people lived such good lives that they became perfect, they united with the cosmic being. Since Ketu belonged to a priestly Brahmin family, everyone believed that he had followed the rules of the Vedas in his last life.

As a child, Ketu learned to recite the names of his male

ancestors beginning with his father and going back many generations. He was proud of his father's family line, but he was also proud that his mother belonged to the second most important class: the Kshatriya, who were the warriors and politicians. (During Vedic times, people from different *varna* could marry, but in later periods this practice was discouraged and eventually banned.)

Ketu walked to the river for his bath with boys from the Vaisya class. Their fathers were merchants and important community leaders. On the road they passed another group of boys who were driving oxen pulling a heavy plow to the fields. These boys were from the lowest class, the Shudra. Shudras worked the land and butchered animals or made leather harnesses. Because the work that they did was considered unclean, they were not allowed to learn the sacred hymns and prayers called **mantras**. They were not even allowed to touch the sacred pottery or containers used to carry the food that would be sacrificed to the gods.

If Ketu even brushed against a Shudra, he had to bathe and purify himself right away. As a Brahmin, his job was to keep the world from ending by making sacrifices to the gods, which he could only do if he was pure. This was the Brahmins' sacred duty, not just for themselves, but for everyone in the community, including the Kshatriyas, Vaisyas, and even the untouchable Shudras. It was an important responsibility. *You* wouldn't want to be responsible for the end of the world, would you?

Ketu was preparing for his initiation along with some other boys from his class. When that day arrived, his mother and sister plastered the courtyard of their home with a fresh layer of clay mixed with sacred cow manure. Cows were holy, and their manure mixed with clay purified the space needed for the special ritual. (Many harmful bacteria do not grow in cow manure, so this practice actually *did* keep things clean. Grass fibers in the manure did something else, too, it made the plaster of the walls stronger.) Ketu's family built a small, square fire altar in the center of the courtyard with four rectangular fired bricks that his mother and sister also plastered with clay and manure.

man + *tra* = "to think" + "tool" or "instrument"
A mantra is a word or saying repeated during meditation or worship. One popular mantra is the word "ohm."

The fire god Agni, often shown with two heads and seven tongues, was considered the mouth of the gods. Worshippers gave him offerings to feed all the gods and keep the world in harmony. This 17th-century carving is from South India.

MAJOR GODS AND GODDESSES OF THE VEDAS	
Agni	*god of fire and sacrifice*
Indra	*god of war and rain*
Saraswati, Ganga, and others	*river goddesses (each major river was a goddess)*
Surya	*sun god*
Ushas	*goddess of the dawn*

66 Hymn to Agni, Rig Veda, 1700 BCE

When everything was ready, Ketu's father and two other priests brought out the special tools to kindle the sacred fire. One man held a wood plank, and a second man held a wooden drill. Ketu's father pulled back and forth on a cord wrapped around the thick wooden drill, so that the drill tip pressed into the wood board. After a few turns, the tip of the stick started to smoke, and soon the charred wood powder that built up in the hearth began to glow. One of the priests blew on the glowing embers and added a bit of dry kindling soaked in butter until the sacred fire—Agni—sprang to life.

Once the fire was going, Ketu's father recited a hymn to Agni, inviting the god to the altar to receive the sacrifice:

May your offerings, oblations, directed to heaven
Come forth with the butter ladle.
Agni goes to the gods, seeking their favor.
Having been called, Agni, sit down for the feast.

Then the priests recited prayers to purify Ketu and the other boys who were sitting quietly in a row next to the fire altar. The boys dropped butter and small animal and human figurines made of wheat flour into the sacred fire. The priests sprinkled purified water over the heads of each boy, and then carefully draped the sacred cotton thread over their left shoulders, around their bodies, and under their right arms. This sacred thread was a symbol of the boys' second birth as Brahmin students. (Kshatriya and Vaisya boys could also receive the sacred thread, but they had to wait until they were older.)

After receiving the sacred thread, Ketu and his friends moved into the house of a learned priest who tutored them for 12 years. A student's life was very hard. Students collected firewood for fire sacrifices and everyday cooking, helped build fire altars, and learned to make the sacred fire. Most of the time, they memorized the Vedas, carefully pronouncing each sound exactly right to call the gods to sacrifices.

Many young boys were not as lucky as Ketu, or even as lucky as the Shudras, the peasants. The Vedic peoples discriminated against the Dasa, a group of people who spoke a different language that did not sound at all like Sanskrit. The Brahmins sometimes made fun of the Dasa and said that they spoke as if they had no noses. (Pinch your nose and see what you would sound like.) The Dasa had wide flat noses and long curly black hair, and the Brahmins claimed they had darker skin and called them uncivilized barbarians, who didn't know how to behave.

The Dasa had, in reality, lived in the region for hundreds of years. Their ancestors in the Indus Valley were the Harappans who had named the rivers and mountains, and had built the cities that now lay abandoned. Although at first the Rig Vedic culture seemed to sweep over the northern plains, many earlier traditions of the Harappans lived on and reemerged in later times.

NOTHING IS TOO GOOD FOR THE GODS

According to the Vedas, Agni the fire god enjoyed sacrifices of horses, bulls, male buffalo, goats, sheep, and sometimes even human beings. (But it wouldn't be considered cheating to use figurines of clay or flour instead of live animals and people.) The horse sacrifice was particularly important. A pure-white male horse was purified, fed, and then allowed to wander for a full year. Wherever it went, the king and his army followed. If it crossed into a neighboring kingdom, the king there either had to submit to the new king or fight to protect his own borders. After a year, the horse was sacrificed. But if this was too much, Agni also liked plainer sacrifices of milk, curds, and butter from the sacred cow, and *soma,* an intoxicating and stimulating drink.

Brahmin boys are sprinkled with holy Ganga River water by a priest during their upanayana, *or sacred thread ceremony. After the ceremony, they will begin formal study of the Vedas and wear the sacred thread over their left shoulders.*

CHAPTER 12

TWO GREAT ADVENTURES
EPIC TRADITIONS

Which of ancient India's treasures would you most like to take home with you? One of those cool carnelian belts? A rope of milky pearls? A personalized seal carved with your name and favorite animals? An intricately inlaid chest of *shisham* wood? Or perhaps a brightly glazed and gracefully shaped ceramic pot?

Many of the people who love ancient India would choose none of those things. They would vote for the stories of the *Mahabharata* and the *Ramayana*, poems that are as widely read and loved today as they were when they were first composed thousands of years ago.

The hero of the *Mahabharata* is a great warrior named Prince Arjuna. He falls in love with Princess Draupadi, and wins her hand in marriage by stringing a massive bow that is too heavy for anyone else to use. Then he uses the bow to shoot out the eye of a golden fish spinning on top of a tall pole, while looking at the fish's reflection in a vat filled with boiling water.

Despite his beautiful wife and fabulous archery skills, Prince Arjuna has a problem. He and his four brothers, the Pandavas, are at war with his cousins, the Kauravas. Arjuna wants to win the war and defeat his evil cousins. But at the same time, he wants to be a good man, and good men don't go around making war on their relatives. In the *Bhagavad Gita*, a poem that is part of the *Mahabharata*, Arjuna tells his charioteer that "conflicting sacred duties confound my reason."

Lucky for Prince Arjuna, his charioteer turns out to be Lord Krishna, who is an **avatar** of the god Vishnu, the god who preserves life. Krishna explains to Arjuna that even though he may not want to hurt his cousins, it's Arjuna's duty—his *dharma*—to do so. Krishna asks Arjuna what he thinks would happen to the world if the gods didn't do their

“ *Bhagavad Gita*, fourth century BCE–fourth century CE

Avatar comes from the Sanskrit word for "descent." An avatar is the form a god or goddess takes when he or she descends, or comes down, to earth and appears to humankind.

duty, and explains that performing his *dharma* is the only path to peace and salvation. Otherwise, he will just be reborn endlessly until he gets it right.

> Without faith in *dharma*,
> men fail to reach me, Arjuna;
> they return to the cycle
> of death and rebirth.

Despite Krishna's advice, Arjuna holds back at a crucial moment of the battle. The day is saved when Krishna jumps into the fray and sends his spinning *chakra*, a flat disk with a razor-sharp edge, slicing through the advancing army of the Kauravas. The poem ends with the words:

> Where Krishna is lord of discipline
> and Arjuna is the archer,
> there do fortune, victory, abundance,
> and morality exist, so I think.

The ancient Ramayana *story about Rama and his loyal wife, Sita, is still presented in theatres in India to help people understand the important religious message of devotion and truth.*

66 *Bhagavad Gita*, fourth century BCE–fourth century CE

66 *Bhagavad Gita*, fourth century BCE–fourth century CE

The *Mahabharata* is an exciting story, a beautiful poem, and an important source of religious teaching. But it is also a historical document that tells us a lot about the Vedic communities at the end of the Vedic Era. For example, in the final battle, the warriors ride in magnificent chariots covered with gold and gems, with tinkling bells and iron-rimmed wheels, calling each other to battle with trumpets made of conch shells. "Tumult echoed through heaven and earth," says the *Mahabharata*. That passage tells us that the Vedic people had horses and chariots, that their artisans knew how to work with iron and gold, and that they had reestablished trade with the coastal villages that collected conch shells. The place names in the poem also remind us that India was being settled along the Ganga and Yamuna River valleys and in the Punjab. Krishna, for example, was from the city of Mathura, on the Yamuna, while the Kaurava brothers were from the city of Hastinapura, on the Ganga.

Archaeologists have found some of the things talked about in the *Mahabharata* and the *Ramayana*. Both of the

66 *Bhagavad Gita*, fourth century BCE–fourth century CE

Lord Krishna, who is often shown with blue skin to indicate he is a form of the god Vishnu, drives Arjuna's war chariot in the final battle of the Mahabharata.

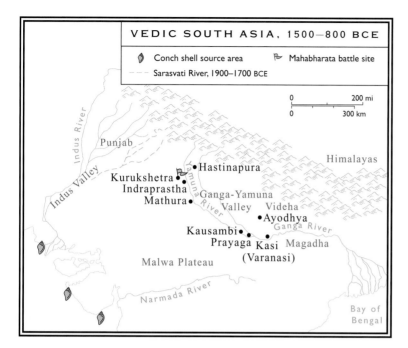

VEDIC SOUTH ASIA, 1500–800 BCE

Conch shell source area   Mahabharata battle site

Sarasvati River, 1900–1700 BCE

0 — 200 mi
0 — 300 km

Indus River

Punjab

Himalayas

Indus Valley

Hastinapura
Kurukshetra
Indraprastha   Ganga-Yamuna
Mathura   Valley   Videha
                        •Ayodhya
Kausambi•   Ganga River
   Prayaga Kasi Magadha
   (Varanasi)

Malwa Plateau

Narmada River

Bay of Bengal

BRONZE AND BRASS

Bronze is made by mixing copper with a little tin and sometimes lead. Add zinc to copper or bronze and you get brass. Combine tin, zinc, or lead with copper and you change its color from reddish to golden—you also make it harder and more brittle. Bronze is good for making weapons and tools as well as for casting fine sculptures. Brass is even easier to cast because it melts at a lower temperature. The Vedic people made perhaps the earliest examples of brass in the world.

poems describe warriors and rulers gambling with dice (the good guys always lose everything because the bad guys cheat!). Sure enough, archaeologists have found colored counters and rod-shaped dice dating from that time—they look a lot like dice still used in India today. They have also found soapstone molds for gold and silver jewelry; horse bones; and iron, brass, and bronze tools.

The *Ramayana* is a Sanskrit poem written by Valmiki sometime between 300 and 200 BCE and based on an episode from the *Mahabharata*, which was composed hundreds of years earlier. The *Ramayana* tells the story of Prince Rama and his lovely wife, Sita. Rama is a good man and a popular leader. Valmiki describes himself as a leader and a father to everyone: "As a father to his children, to his loving men he came." Unfortunately, Rama's father had two families—one with Rama and his mother and brother, and another with Rama's stepmother, Kaikeyi, and her son, Bharata. The king is about to name Rama as his heir when Kaikeyi reminds the king that he has promised that he will grant her two wishes. She wants the king to send Rama into exile for 14 years and to make her son, Bharata, the crown prince.

❝ Valmiki, *Ramayana*, 300–200 BCE

And You Thought You Had a Hard Time Waking Up

Near the end of the Rama-yana, *the villain Ravana decides to ask his brother Kumbakarna for help:*

It was a mighty task to wake up Kumbakarna. A small army had to be engaged. They sounded trumpets and drums at his ears and were ready with enormous quantities of food and drink for him, for when Kumbakarna awoke from sleep, his hunger was phenomenal and he made a meal of whomever he could grab at his bedside. They cudgeled, belabored, pushed, pulled, and shook him, with the help of elephants; at last he opened his eyes and swept his arms about and crushed quite a number among those who had stirred him up.

While Rama is in exile with his wife, Sita, and his younger brother, Lakshmana, an evil ten-headed demon named Ravana captures Sita and takes her to his palace. Rama and his brother spend the next 14 years searching for her, eventually helped by an army from the kingdom of the monkeys. (Monkeys are considered sacred throughout most of South Asia because of the help they gave Rama and Sita.)

The bravest and the cleverest of the monkeys is Hanuman. Hanuman helps Rama find Sita and tries to rescue her from Ravana. In the process, he is captured and forced to sit

Rama sits on the shoulders of the monkey hero Hanuman and aims an arrow at the 10-headed demon Ravana. After killing Ravana, Rama rescues his wife, Sita, and returns to his capital city, Ayodhya.

Bandar Poonch, which means "the mountain of the monkey's tail," is the tallest mountain on the right. The mountain gets its name from a story in the Ramayana.

at the feet of the demon king Ravana. Hanuman uses his coiled tail to lift himself up until he is as high as the king's throne. Each time the king raises his throne to be higher than the captured monkey, Hanuman lifts himself higher with his tail. In the end, the demons are so angry that they tie an oil-soaked rag to his tail and light it on fire. Hanuman races through the palace lighting the whole building on fire before he flies to the snowy Himalayas and buries his burning tail in the snow of a high mountain. When he gets up to leave, he ends up pulling down the top of the mountain. Today the mountain is called Bandar Poonch—the mountain of the Monkey's Tail.

In the end, Rama and Ravana fight a huge battle that spills over into the heavens:

> Rama sent a crescent-shaped arrow which sliced off one of Ravana's heads and flung it far into the sea, and this process continued; but every time a head was cut off, another one grew in its place. Rama lopped off his arms but they grew again and every lopped-off arm hit Matali and the chariot and tried to cause destruction by itself, and the tongue in a new head wagged, uttered challenges, and cursed Rama.

❝ Valmiki, *Ramayana*, 300–200 BCE

Rama eventually triumphs, and everything ends happily, with Sita and Rama reunited and Rama crowned as king. The monkey king Hanuman loved Rama so much that it is said that he is present every time the *Ramayana* is told. So look around—see any monkeys?

CHAPTER 13

NEW GODS
FROM BRAHMANISM
TO EARLY HINDUISM

❝ *Brahmavaivarta Purana,
800–1000 CE*

In Sanskrit, *karma* means
both "action" and "fate."
Karma is the consequence
decided by what you
do today.

*This carving of Vishnu shows the deity
with four arms holding symbols of his
power: a mace, chakra, and conch shell.*

❝All creatures from Brahma to the small insect have to face the result of their deeds," said the Vedic god Vishnu. If you were a student who never practiced your Vedas, or a farmer who let your land go to seed, or a craftsman who sold leaky pots, your parents or your wife or your customers would probably get angry with you. But that's not all. What Vishnu meant was that you could pay in your *next* life for not meeting your duties in *this* one. Your actions had results, which were called *karma*. Many ancient South Asians believed that most people's souls came back into the world after they died, and not necessarily in a human body. If you had earned bad karma, you might come back as a chicken, a fish, or a pig. Many ancient South Asians did not eat anything that flew, walked, or swam. Even a mosquito had a soul.

On the other hand, if you were especially good, you could come back as a Brahmin. Brahmins were considered to be the most pure of all human beings. Only they knew the hymns and rituals from the Vedas to call the gods and goddesses to the fire sacrifice. They knew how to start a fire with a bow drill and, once that fire was started, how to offer sacrificed animals and clarified butter (or "ghee") to the flames as they chanted special hymns.

By around 1000 BCE, the Vedic rituals practiced by Brahmins began to change. Earlier traditions of the Indus civilization and other local beliefs began to creep back into use. The Brahmins began to use Harappan-style conch-shell ladles to pour sacrifices and blow Harappan-style conch shells to call the gods. They began to practice the ancient Harappan discipline of yoga and decorate the floors where they performed rituals with sacred designs called *mandalas*, made out of powdered conch shells and rice powder.

A person who could call the gods to sacrifice was a very special person indeed. But probably the best thing about being a Brahmin was that Brahmins were the closest to reaching the Ultimate Supreme Being, called *brahman*. When people who had lived perfectly died, they stopped being individuals and united with *brahman*. South Asians looked forward to uniting with *brahman* so that they could stop the endless cycle of death and rebirth. But even if you were a Brahmin, there were no guarantees. If a Brahmin lived a bad life that resulted in bad karma, he could live his next life as a worm.

Still, being good was not enough to be **reincarnated** as a human, never mind to reach the level of *brahman*. You also had to purify yourself through special rituals. People tried to wash away the sins that they committed during their life through rituals such as bathing in sacred rivers, singing hymns to the gods and goddesses, giving alms to

Sacred geometric designs, or man-dalas, such as this endless knot design, are prepared by women to welcome the gods and confuse evil spirits. Each day, women make new designs with powdered conch shell, rice flour, or colorful paints.

Reincarnation is from the Latin word, *incarnare*, meaning "to make flesh." To be reincarnated means to be reborn into a new body.

Brahma is still being worshipped today in many parts of India. On this 11th-century sculpture two other faces of Brahma are seen in profile.

the poor and to charitable organizations, and taking care of old and weak animals as well as people. They gave away all their wealth, devoted themselves to meditation, and made pilgrimages to sacred places.

Many of these sacred places were found along the shores of India's Ganges, or Ganga, River. Just as the Indus Valley civilization grew from the life-giving waters of the Indus and Saraswati Rivers, so the Brahmanical religion grew up along the banks of the Ganga River. The people of ancient South Asia thought of the river as a beautiful goddess. According to the *Ramayana*, "[The] Ganga [river is] flowing along the valley, coming down from the Himalayas, carrying within her the essence of rare herbs and elements found on her way. She courses through many a kingdom, and every inch of the ground she touches becomes holy."

The Ganga River may physically spring from the Himalaya Mountains, but according to some ancient South Asian myths, this goddess cascades from the top of a god's head. That god is Shiva, lord of creation and destruction, and beginning in about 1000 BCE he joined Brahma and Vishnu as one of the three major gods. Powerful Shiva is made up of the forces of the universe, according to some scriptures called the *Upanishads*:

Ramayana, 300–200 BCE

Mundaka Upanishad, 700–300 BCE

Fire is in his forehead, the sun and moon are his eyes, the directions of space are his ears, the Veda is his voice, the wind that pervades the world is the breath which raises his chest, his feet are the earth. He is the inner self of all living beings.

Shiva has three eyes, which represent the sun, the moon, and a Supreme Force. When he opens his eye of Supreme Force, a flash of fire destroys his enemies, and blesses the good with wisdom. Shiva holds a trident, a three-pronged weapon to kill evil demons, in one hand and a conch shell in the other. The conch shell comes from the bones of a demon named Shankhachuda, whom Shiva

MAJOR HINDU GODS AND GODDESSES		
Brahma	*god of creation*	*holds the four Vedas, a pot for ritual cleansing, prayer beads and a conch shell*
Shiva	*god of fertility*	*has a third eye to destroy evil*
Vishnu	*the "Preserver"*	*appears in ten different human forms, including Krishna*
Ganesha	*god of wisdom, remover of obstacles, elephant-headed son of Shiva and Parvati*	*holds a rod to clear obstacles from mankind's path*
Lakshmi	*goddess of beauty, luck, and wealth, also mother goddess, Vishnu's partner*	*carries lotus and swastika, which symbolize good luck and wealth*
Ganga	*mother and river goddess, Shiva's partner*	*rides a crocodile*
Parvati	*mother and protector goddess, Shiva's wife and Ganesha's mother*	*carries prayer beads, a mirror, bell, and a lime, which is a symbol of fertility; rides a tiger or lion*
Kali	*mother goddess and destroyer of evil, Shiva's partner*	*wears a necklace of the skulls of those she has destroyed*
Saraswati	*mother and river goddess, also goddess of wisdom and music, Vishnu's partner*	*plays a stringed instrument called a vina*
Surya	*sun god, life giver*	*rides in a chariot with seven horses*

destroyed with the help of the god Vishnu. The shell represents Shiva's power. Not only does Shiva have one more eye than humans do, he is often described as having many hands that represent different aspects of his power. His hands may hold an axe to cut off the heads of evil demons; prayer beads; or a small drum for dancing. Shiva loves to dance, which represents the way the universe is always moving. Since he is responsible for death as well as life, he is often shown wearing snakes, which are symbols of death and decay, as is the waning crescent moon he wears in his piled and matted hair.

Shiva wears a pair of mismatched earrings. This jewelry represents his masculine side and his feminine side. The one in his right ear is in the shape of a crocodile-like creature. That one represents his masculine nature. His other earring is circular with a hole in the middle. It represents his feminine nature. Sometimes Shiva is shown half male and half female to symbolize fertility. And sometimes Shiva is completely female. Then Shiva is known as Devi or the Mother Goddess. Devi changes her form depending on the circumstance. She can be either destructive or loving and gentle. Durga and Kali are terrible and extremely bloodthirsty forms of this goddess. Although they seem frightening, Durga and Kali are not out to get good people. They are there to destroy evil and demons. The Mother Goddess may also appear as Lakshmi, the goddess of wealth and prosperity, and Saraswati, the goddess of learning and music.

Shiva was not the only god that people began paying more attention to about 1000 BCE. People began telling more and more stories about Vishnu. Vishnu takes on a special form (called an avatar) and appears on earth to save people whenever some major obstacle or evil power threatens the universe. Krishna, who drives the chariot of Prince Arjuna in the *Mahabharata*, is actually Vishnu appearing as

Shiva often has many arms to show his power of creation and destruction. The Ganga River flows from his head, and the humped bull Nandi waits on him. He wears a necklace made from the heads of the many demons he has conquered.

a charioteer in order to lead the embattled prince to victory. Vishnu's job is to maintain the balance between good and evil in the universe. From time to time, it becomes necessary for Vishnu to destroy the universe, because there is too much evil and it has to be purified. But after a period of rest, the whole cycle of existence begins again.

In sculpture, Vishnu often has four hands, each holding a symbol of his power. In one hand he holds a conch shell which, just like Shiva's, symbolizes his power. In another hand, he wields a razor-sharp disk, a weapon that symbolizes the way intelligence can destroy all evil (the disk is called a *chakra*). In another hand, Vishnu holds a lotus, a flower that grows in water. Lotuses are rooted in mud but they blossom above the water. Vishnu's lotus is a symbol of his creative force and lordship over the universe. In his fourth hand, Vishnu holds a club or mace, which is a symbol of his power and knowledge.

Shiva and Vishnu often accompany Brahma. Brahma, who should not be confused with *brahman*, the Ultimate Supreme Being, is the oldest of the three major Hindu gods. Although all three gods are mentioned in the Vedas, Shiva and Vishnu didn't become really popular until later. In the *Ramayana*, Brahma himself says that "Of the Trinity, I am the Creator, Shiva is the Destroyer, and Vishnu is the Protector."

Brahma rides a swan or goose to symbolize purity, detachment, and divine knowledge, and Vishnu and Shiva usually accompany him. Brahma represents the balance between forces that destroy and fragment the universe and those that create and unite. He is usually shown with four heads, facing north, south, east, and west, so that he can see everything (at one point he actually had a fifth head, but that was cut off by Shiva during a fight). His heads also represent the four Vedas and the four groups that people are divided into (called *varnas*). He is often shown with four arms that hold symbolic objects: a special pot with a spout that is used for ritual cleansing and represents the earth, the sustainer of all things; palm-leaf manuscripts, which represent the Vedas; prayer beads that he uses to recite prayers; and the sacred conch shell that calls the gods to sacrifices.

Ramayana, 300–200 BCE

RISE AND SHINE!

After starting breakfast, a Brahmin girl would help her mother with the daily household rituals. Using either white rice flour or ground conch shell, she would draw complex, mazelike designs in doorways and on steps. These drawings, called *mandalas*, were meant to welcome good spirits, and to capture and confuse evil spirits. Then she and her mother would light a sacred lamp to the goddess who protected their home. They would anoint the figure of the goddess with brilliant red vermilion powder, then dip their second littlest fingers into the lamp's oil, then into the red pigment, and carefully apply a red dot in the middle of their foreheads. This red dot symbolized their purity and association with the goddess. Once all these rituals were completed, it was time to wake the men.

Back among mere mortals, the Brahmin men—and only the Brahmin men—were taught the sacred scriptures and conducted sacrifices. And that was the main job they were born to do. If they took on some other responsibility, they could ruin their chances of joining *brahman*. In early Vedic times, every kind of responsibility was delegated to a particular group, or *varna*. For example, people of the Kshatriya group owned land, fought wars, and ran the government. The members of the Vaisya *varna* became craftsmen and traders. The Shudra group worked the land, swept the streets, emptied the latrines, and collected garbage and dumped it outside the city. Although at first it was possible for people to move from one *varna* to another, changing places was discouraged, and after about 1000 BCE, it was not allowed at all.

Based on what *varna* you were born into, your career was decided for you. Any say you had in the matter was narrowed even further by whether you were a boy or a girl. Brahmin boys learned the rituals and scriptures that their fathers, brothers, and uncles did. Brahmin girls and women fed and clothed their families and cared for the young, the elderly, and the sick. They also performed religious rituals, especially the daily worship of the goddess who protects

The three most important Hindu gods—Brahma, Vishnu, and Shiva—appear, from left to right, on this 19th-century painting. Brahma and Saraswati, the goddess of knowledge and music, ride Hamsa the swan. Vishnu and Lakshmi, the goddess of good fortune and prosperity, sit on Garuda, who is half-man, half-eagle. And Shiva and Parvati, the goddess of childbirth, ride the white bull Nandi. They are followed by Shiva and Parvati's son, Ganesha, the elephant-headed god of good luck, and Hanuman.

the home and family. Many aspects of women's worship was not part of the early Vedic scriptures—it was handed down from mother to daughter from very ancient times.

We don't know very much about women and men from the lower classes, because the records we have, the Vedas, the *Mahabharata*, and the *Ramayana*, are about the upper classes. Many scholars believe that the need to earn a living meant that men and women worked together more equally among the other classes than they did among the Brahmins. Non-Brahmin women were allowed and even encouraged to get an education and sometimes were trained in warfare.

The earlier Vedic religion was changing. Animal sacrifices were being replaced with butter and fruit offerings, new gods were emphasized instead of Agni and Brahma, and people couldn't move between the *varnas* at all. In time, these new practices became known as **Hinduism**.

But not everyone found meaning and comfort in sacrifices and strict social divisions. By the sixth century BCE, two young men were struggling to find gentler, more peaceable ways of finding God. Their names were Mahavira and Siddhartha Gautama, and their efforts would give birth to two of the world's great religions, Jainism and Buddhism.

Hindu, from the word *Indus*, is the 19th-century British name for non-Muslim South Asians. Today, Hindu refers to people who believe in reincarnation and worship gods and goddesses like Vishnu, Shiva, and Devi. Hinduism isn't so much a single unified religion as a family of religious traditions.

CHAPTER 14

TWO GENTLE RELIGIONS
BUDDHISM AND JAINISM

Finding Peace

Early Hinduism taught people to find peace by controlling their desires. In the Bhagavad Gita, *for example, Krishna explains that*

As the mountainous
  depths of the ocean
are unmoved when
  waters rush into it,
So the man unmoved
  when desires enter him
  attains a peace that eludes
  the man of many desires.

Sometime during the sixth century BCE, a prince named Vardamana was born in northern India. His father was a Kshatriya and his mother's family controlled much of what is now Nepal and Eastern India. As the son of a powerful ruler, he lived a life of luxury. Wealth and pleasures surrounded him. He married and had a daughter, but when he was 30 years old, he began to feel bored and trapped by his life and all of his things. He decided to leave the palace and, after tearing out his hair in five handfuls, he began to wander the land, meditating, and living off the food that people gave him.

He traveled into faraway forests, where he met holy men and women who, like him, disliked the violence and greed of ordinary life. Together they looked for a better way to live. In time, Vardamana found out about a holy man who had lived hundreds of year before, in about 800 BCE. This man, whose name was Prashavanatha, taught that as long as you did not lie, steal, own more than you needed to survive, or kill anything, your life would be pure and you would be freed from having to be born yet again.

Vardamana began to follow these teachings, living only off the charity that people gave him. Sometimes people beat and abused him, but he stuck to his beliefs. Finally, after 12 years, 6 months and 15 days, he was able to conquer his earthly desires. He no longer cared about fancy food, fashionable clothes, or even his family and friends. He had finally reached a state called Enlightenment—the burden of always wanting stuff didn't weigh him down anymore. People called him Mahavira, "the great hero." He taught the four teachings of Prashavanatha, plus one more: celibacy. Total celibacy was a tough one, since if no one had children, people would die out. So, many people who followed the teachings of Vardamana gave up worldly pleasures after they had finished raising a family.

One of the main messages that drew people to the teachings of Mahavira was his idea that all things are connected:

> All men who are ignorant of the Truth are subject to pain; in the endless cycle of rebirth they suffer in many ways.
>
> Therefore a wise man, who considers well the ways that lead to bondage and birth, should himself search for the truth, and be kind towards all creatures.

Discourses of Mahavira, 600–500 BCE

Mahavira's five rules of telling the truth, never stealing, never owning anything, never hurting anything, and remaining celibate were very difficult to follow. But in time his teachings became popular anyway. Most everyone wanted to reach *moksha*, release from the cycle of rebirth. People believed that Mahavira achieved *moksha* upon his death at the age of 72. Instead of being born again, his spirit united with the universe. Some said that Indra, king of the gods, collected the pieces of his bones that were left after his body was burned and took them to heaven, where the gods joined together to worship them.

Mahavira did not try to start a religion. He was one of many teachers who had conquered the senses—who had learned how not to pay attention to feelings such as hunger, thirst, and pain—and helped others to understand the way to reach *moksha*. Mahavira and others who have conquered their five senses are called *jina*, or conquerors. The name of the religious tradition that grew up around these teachers is called Jainism.

In Jainism, men and women who are great teachers are called "ford makers." A ford is a place where it is easy to cross a stream— a ford maker is someone who helps others find a way to cross from the river of life and endless

Jain nuns on a pilgrimage wear masks over their mouths and noses so they don't swallow insects by mistake. Jains are forbidden from killing any creature, no matter how small.

death and rebirth, to the peace of enlightenment, when the soul unites with the universe. These teachers learned to control their senses and desires and to break free from life on Earth. Mahavira was the 24th ford maker.

Both men and women who admired Mahavira and his teachings left their families and became monks and nuns. In fact, when Mahavira died, more than twice as many nuns as monks followed his teachings. Even today, women play an important role in Jain traditions. As mothers, they teach children how to behave and how to live a good life by not killing, stealing, or lying. Jain nuns meditate and go on journeys called pilgrimages to sacred places, take care of sacred scriptures, and teach others about the way to achieve Enlightenment.

All Jains vow not to kill any living thing. This means that Jains cannot be farmers, because they would have to kill insects that destroy plants and they would kill worms when plowing the fields. Jains do not raise animals because they would have to kill the lice, vermin, and germs that livestock often suffer from. They can't be lumberjacks, because that line of work would mean that by cutting down trees they would be killing insects and hurting animals that live in the trees.

Most Jains who were not monks and nuns were traders, bankers, or craftspeople who made things such as jewelry and cloth. The rich Jain merchants became patrons of the arts and paid for the construction of magnificent temples and monasteries. Many of the teachings of famous monks and nuns were written on palm leaves or painted onto birch-bark manuscripts and collected in great libraries.

Not all followers of Jain traditions practice the strict rules that Mahavira laid out. At first, Jain teaching did not allow people to worship statues or paintings of gods, a common practice among early Hindus, or even to worship in temples. But in time, a few Jains began to take on some of the traditions of the early Hindus. Around the first century CE, Jains began building temples with stories illustrating the lives of their saints carved in stone. In the fifth century CE, Jains began to build white marble temples with golden

Most early documents in South Asia have not survived because they were written on fragile materials such as birch bark, palm leaf, or cloth. This rare birch-bark manuscript in Brahmi script from 400 CE was found in a dry cave in Pakistan.

spires and even began offering sacrifices to their ford makers. Because Jains did not believe in animal sacrifice, they offered gifts of flowers and fruit to the gods and decorated their statues with a paste made from sweet-smelling sandalwood. The largest Jain image today is a huge—about 20 feet (18 meters) tall—statue of a saint in South India. On special occasions, thousands of gallons of milk, sweet-smelling wood and spices, and bright red vermilion, a red powder that stands for purity, are poured over the statue's head and allowed to run down its body. Then pilgrims collect the leftover offerings and use them to wash their bodies. They believe this will purify them.

At about the same time as Mahavira was wandering around the forest and cities of the Ganga Valley, another prince was asking similar questions. His name was Siddhartha Gautama. Like Mahavira's father, Siddhartha's father tried

Statue of Jain saint Gomatesvara, South India, 983 CE

Each year, pilgrims climb onto this statue of Gomatesvara and pour over it clarified butter, or ghee, to commemorate the anniversary of the saint's death.

to protect him from anything ugly or painful. Like Mahavira, Siddhartha married and had a child. And like Mahavira, Siddhartha gradually realized that the world was a place of suffering. He gave up his life of luxury, left his palace, and began to seek enlightenment. Buddhists believe that after six years of fasting and long periods of meditating in the same position without moving a muscle, he realized that physical discipline was not the way to achieve enlightenment. When he told this to five fellow sages, they left him in the forest, disgusted that he had given up so easily. But Siddhartha continued to meditate. One night, as he sat on a grass mat under the arching branches of a bodhi (wild fig) tree, he realized something that would change his life forever. It occurred to Siddhartha that

66 Buddha, The Four Noble Truths, fifth–fourth centuries BCE

1) humans experience pain

2) desire or wanting is what causes this pain

3) the only way to avoid suffering is to control desire

4) a person can be freed from desire, and achieve Enlightenment, by living with others and following the **Eightfold Path**.

Also known as the Middle Path. The eight ways to freedom from desire are in taking the right view, resolve, speech, action, living, effort, mindfulness, and meditation.

Siddhartha called this form of enlightenment Nirvana. Once he experienced Nirvana for himself, he became known as the Buddha.

Although he did not think anyone would be interested in his message, he decided to share what he had discovered. At the town of Sarnath, the five friends who had abandoned him in the forest came to listen to him teach. These five became his first followers. For the next 45 years, the Buddha traveled from city to city and village to village, teaching people about kindness, compassion, and truth, as he did in these instructions to one of his followers:

66 Buddha, *Admonition to Singala*, fifth–fourth centuries BCE

The wise and moral man
Shines like a fire on a hilltop
Making honey like a bee
Who does not hurt the flower.

Prince Siddhartha rides to school in a cart pulled by rams in this stone sculpture. He is surrounded by royal servants who protected him from seeing pain and suffering in the world. Later, he left his royal surroundings to search for the truth and gain enlightenment.

He did not speak in the fancy Sanskrit used by Brahmin priests, but instead in simple, easy-to-understand words in the local languages. He quickly became very popular and had soon gathered a large following, called a *sangha*—a community. His followers included princes and common people, kings, and farmers—inside of the *sangha*, no one bothered about *varna*, or class. When Buddha died at the age of 80, he was cremated and his ashes were distributed and buried in dome-shaped monuments called stupas. His followers continued his work. They wore simple yellow robes and traveled around the country eight months of the year preaching the Four Noble Truths that the Buddha had taught them.

The Buddha preached Four Noble Truths that helped a person gain release from the process of rebirth. This ultimate freedom is called *nirvana*. It is a state in which the individual's sense of him- or herself ceases to exist and there is nothing to be reborn. Instead of focusing on "me" and "mine," a person who follows the teachings of Buddha begins to learn how to focus on "everything and nothing" at the same time.

Early Buddhist religious practices stayed away from what they thought were difficult and snobby rituals and costly sacrifices. Simple rituals included meditation, pilgrimages, and offerings of food to pilgrims. Eventually, faithful Buddhists began to build burial monuments, meditation halls, monasteries, and sacred monuments to remind each other about the Buddha and his teachings.

By the third century BCE, even kings and queens were beginning to adopt the simple ways of Buddhism. In about 261 BCE, Emperor Ashoka, ruler of the Mauryan empire in India, converted to Buddhism and made it the state religion of his empire. He had stone columns and tablets carved with Buddhist ideas, such as "In India the gods who formerly did not mix with men now do so. This is the result of effort, and may be obtained not only by the great, but even by the small, through effort—thus they may even easily win heaven." Ashoka also built *stupas*, dome-shaped burial monuments, to house portions of the Buddha's ashes.

With Ashoka's help, Buddhism spread throughout the subcontinent and beyond, along the major sea and overland trade routes. Some traditions say that Ashoka's son became a monk and his father sent him as a missionary to Sri Lanka, an island off the coast of India. More missionaries traveled to Central Asia, Tibet and China, as well as Southeast Asia, where they converted many people to the gentle teachings of the Buddha.

After the Buddha's death, tiny bits of his ashes were placed in small caskets and sent to many parts of the world. The caskets were buried in gigantic domed monuments called stupas. This stupa is in Swat, Pakistan.

" Ashokan Rock Edict, third century BCE

DON'T JUST DO SOME-THING—SIT THERE!

The earliest images of people meditating are found on the seals of the Indus Valley, dating to around 2500 BCE. During the Vedic period, people believed that the god Shiva practiced yoga to concentrate his energy and connect all of his sacred power.

The word *yoga* means "connecting" or "harnessing" power. It is a series of breathing and stretching exercises that calm and strengthen the body. People from the major religious traditions of South Asia—Hindu, Jain, and Buddhist—practice yoga or meditation. This description of yoga is from the *Bhagavad Gita*: He shuns external objects / fixes his gaze between his brows / and regulates his vital breaths / as they pass through his nostrils.

CHAPTER 15

WORD FOR WORD
EARLY HISTORIC CITIES

I n 1819, a young man named James Prinsep boarded a ship near his home in Essex, England, and set sail for India, half a world away. His father, John, had made the family's fortune manufacturing **indigo** there 40 years earlier, and James had grown up listening to his father's romantic stories of the faraway land. James had raced through his education as quickly as he could, eager to get to India and see it for himself. Now 20 years old and fully qualified as an architect, he was at last on his way.

John Prinsep, James's father, had brought the first Western-style coin-making machinery to India in 1780 and manufactured copper coins to make doing business easier. (Before this, each Indian state had made and used its own hand-stamped coins.) James got a job in Calcutta at the **mint** his father had established. He was good at his job. He reformed the system of weights and measures and introduced a style of coinage that came to be used by the entire country.

In his spare time, James became interested in archaeology. His love for old coins and enthusiasm for anything to do with ancient India was contagious. Many Englishmen living in India began to study Indian history more seriously (including a young man named Alexander Cunningham, the same Alexander Cunningham who would later discover the ruins at Harappa.) Soon James had friends, both English and Indian, sending him old coins and copies of inscriptions from all over India.

James spent hours admiring the portraits of long-forgotten kings that decorated his old coins. Some of his oldest coins dated from the time of Alexander the Great, when the **Indo-Greeks** ruled northern India and Pakistan. Those coins had inscriptions in ancient Greek on one side, which he could decipher. But the meaning of the inscriptions on the other side, which were written in a mysterious squiggly

{ *Indigo* is from the Latin *indicum*, which means "Indian substance." Indigo is the plant used to dye blue jeans, or denim.

{ *Mint* is from the Latin *moneta*, which means "money." A mint is a place where coins are manufactured and paper money is printed.

{ "Indo" is from the Latin *Indus*, meaning "Indian." The Indo-Greeks were people from Greece who had settled in India.

alphabet scholars called Brahmi, baffled him. He thought they probably repeated the Greek information, but until someone could read Brahmi, there was no way to be sure.

James began to make lists of the kings he found on the coins, trying to put them in some kind of chronological order. Part way through that project, James moved to

 Indo-Greek coin, Pakistan, 170–145 BCE

Greek rulers in Bactria and the northern Indus Valley issued coins with their own images on one side and the figure of a god on the other. This silver coin features Eucratides the Great on one side and the twin sons of the Greek mythological queen Leda on the other.

Benares, in northeast India, to open a new mint (in a building he had designed). Benares is close to many important Buddhist sites. As James traveled among them, he found more examples of the same Brahmi script carved into rock pillars and monuments. His desire to decipher Brahmi became an obsession.

He noticed that some short inscriptions on one particular Buddhist stupa, or burial ground, all ended with the same two letters. James guessed that the inscriptions might be offerings, and that the letters might stand for the Sanskrit word *danam*, which means "gift." He had made many similar guesses before, and none of them had panned out, but this time he was right. Thrilled to be getting somewhere at last, James worked feverishly day and night for months until he had cracked the Brahmi alphabet. Then he collapsed from overwork. His health broken, James was forced to leave India.

Why did deciphering Brahmi matter so much to this talented young man? That's easy. James Prinsep knew that once archaeologists could read Brahmi, they would be able to recover whole chapters of India's past that had previously

 Brahmi inscription, Sanchi, 3rd century CE

been locked away behind unreadable inscriptions. For example, historians knew the names the Greeks had used for South Asian kings, but those names didn't appear in South Asian stories and legends. Prinsep thought that perhaps some of the Greek records and South Asian stories were using different names to describe the same people. It's bad enough not to be able to know about prehistoric times. But to have documents and inscriptions in your hand that might be able to answer all your questions if only you knew how to read them—well, that was enough to drive anyone to more work than was good for him.

Sadly, James Prinsep died soon after returning home to England, before many of the questions that had tortured him could be answered. But, largely as a result of the work he and his network of English and Indian friends had done, new knowledge about South Asia's history came quickly.

Most of this knowledge was about South Asia from about 800–300 BCE, a time when people were moving from outposts in the jungle and the deserts into settled communities. As these new towns and cities grew, so did the demand for metals for tools and ornaments. Metalworkers invented new technologies that allowed them to make steel, which made stronger, lighter tools and weapons that didn't rust. Diamond-tipped drills made drilling beads faster and easier. Traders and merchants pushed into previously unexplored territories in search of new sources of gold, silver, copper, and iron.

Sailors carried goods to Sri Lanka from the Indus delta on the west coast and the Yamuna and Ganga deltas to the east. For the first time, coastal communities from both the east and west coasts of the Indian subcontinent, previously separated by dense forests and jungles, could communicate and trade with each other. From Sri Lanka, the sailors continued along the coasts of Southeast Asia, Arabia, and northern Africa.

Buddhist pilgrims carved this stupa design on a boulder along the Indus River near Pakistan about 2,000 years ago. Many such carvings included prayers for a safe passage and the names of people who gave donations to help the pilgrims along the way.

MONEY AND MEASURES

The earliest punch-marked silver coins in South Asia copied silver-bar coins used by the Persians. However, the weights of the coins were the same as the stone weights the people of the Indus Valley had used for hundreds of years. The continuity of this weight system may have been due to the common use of the red and black seed of the jungle plant called *gunja* as a unit of weight.

Both traders and the goods they produced were also moving overland into Central Asia and Iran, where Cyrus the Great of Persia (558–529 BCE) was busily assembling the largest empire the world had ever known. After conquering the northwestern region of the Indus Valley and Afghanistan, Cyrus made it a satrapy, a state within his empire, governed by a **satrap**. The satrap's task as governor was to keep an eye on things and collect taxes, which were sent to the royal capital at Persepolis.

Becoming part of the Persian Empire had a profound impact on the people of South Asia. For one thing, their young men were drafted into the Persian army to fight the Greeks. As these young men traveled throughout the Persian Empire and Greece, they saw new products—such

In Old Persian, *satrap* means "protector of his country."

According to legend, Taxila was founded by Bharata, Rama's half-brother, and named after his son Taksha. The first performance of the Mahabharata is also supposed to have taken place in Taxila.

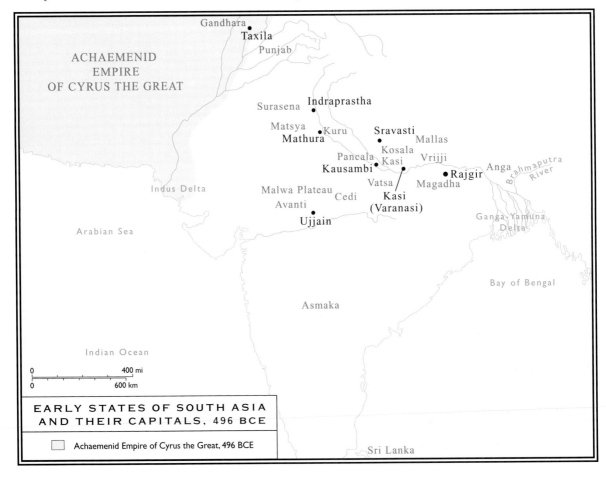

EARLY STATES OF SOUTH ASIA
AND THEIR CAPITALS, 496 BCE

☐ Achaemenid Empire of Cyrus the Great, 496 BCE

This fragment of a stone column is inscribed with Brahmi script, which was first used to write local languages called Prakrit. The script was later used to write Sanskrit.

as wine, musical instruments, and carved gemstones. And they saw new ways of doing things—such as organized athletics and different styles of dress—some of which they wanted for themselves. At the same time, Persian and Greek-speaking soldiers and officials from Iran and Central Asia were sent to the city of Taxilia to administer the cities of the northern Indus Valley. These new settlers also brought Greek and Persian ideas to their new home, including coins with pictures of gods and rulers on them.

Caravans from China, Greece, Persia, and the Indus Valley all passed through Taxila, which quickly became a wealthy center for trade. Buddhist and Brahmanical monasteries and temples, schools and universities, and beautiful royal gardens dotted the city and its outskirts. Rulers and ministers throughout the subcontinent sent their sons to the university at Taxila to be taught the Vedas and the traditional Indian arts and sciences, including archery, swordsmanship, medicine, law, economics, astronomy, mathematics, and literature. For example, a collection of stories about the Buddha called the *Jataka Tales* tells this story about Brahmadatta, King of Benares:

> Now kings of former times . . . used to send their sons to foreign countries afar off to complete their education, that by this means they might learn to quell their pride and high-mindedness, and endure heat or cold, and be made acquainted with the ways of the world. So did this king. Calling his boy to him—now the lad was sixteen years old—he gave him one-soled sandals, a sunshade of leaves, and a thousand pieces of money, with these words: "My son, get you to Taxila, and study there."

THE RETURN OF THE CITIES

1500–800 BCE
Cities develop in Ganga Valley

800–300 BCE
Brahmi script spreads throughout South Asia; cities are established

---

558–529 BCE
Cyrus the Great rules Persia

---

518 BCE
Persian emperor Darius makes Taxila capital of Indian portion of Persian empire

---

486–465 BCE
Reign of Persian emperor Xerxes; Persians conquer central Indus Valley and the Punjab

---

❝ *Jataka Tales*, eighth–third centuries BCE

FINALLY, SOME PEACE AND QUIET

When people from the early cities wanted to get away from the hustle and bustle of urban life, they went to an ashram. An ashram is a hermitage, or a place to meditate and get away from the city. The early cities had large suburbs interspersed with forests, fields, and grazing land. The ashrams were often located in the forests, along the river or in the midst of quiet gardens, with tanks of water filled with lotus and water lilies. Large shade trees such as the sacred fig, or bodhi tree, served as outdoor meeting areas.

Holy men, such as Mahavira and Buddha, would have spent much of their time in these secluded and quiet spots, meditating under the trees and preaching to people who gathered to hear them. Much later, these same secluded spots would become built up with temples and stupas.

Sometimes big cities make it easier for people from different backgrounds to come together. That was *not* the case during this period in South Asia. Instead, people grouped themselves into strict neighborhoods. Over time, the four basic *varnas* (Brahmin priests, Kshatriya warriors, Vaisya artisans, and the lower-class Shudra) had been further subdivided into job-based groups, or castes—for example, jewelers, bakers, and leather workers. Even travelers were expected to honor the divisions of caste. In later times, there were special rest houses for foreigners and travelers who might be from different castes.

Buying and selling became much easier once everyone started using the same kind of coins. The Indo-Greeks also adopted a system of weights that was almost identical to the Indus weight system of the previous millennium. At the same time, each kingdom or republic began to use silver or copper coins with images of kings, gods, and symbols stamped on them, just like the Greek coins they had admired so much. James Prinsep never knew that many of the problems he tried to solve at his job at the mint—finding a common currency and weights and measures—had already been solved, and in remarkably similar way, by the men and women over whose Brahmi alphabet he labored each night.

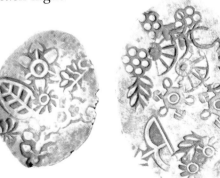

Punch-marked coins, Banaras, India, 500–300 BCE

Early Indian rulers used religious symbols and royal identification marks on their coins instead of images of kings or gods. When coins were taken from one city to another, additional stamps certified that they were the correct weight and of high-quality silver.

CHAPTER 16

WITH FRIENDS LIKE THESE, WHO NEEDS ENEMIES?

THE BEGINNINGS OF THE MAURYAN EMPIRE

“ ARRIAN, FIRDAUSI, AND KAUTILYA

It was the summer of 327 BCE, and Ambhi, king of Taxila, was not a happy camper. For one thing, Taxila was no longer as powerful and wealthy as it had been when the Persians ruled there. He was glad the Persians had gone, of course. Every once in a while, they'd send someone around asking for taxes, but as long as he paid them, the Persians pretty much left King Ambhi and his people alone. Nevertheless, he probably wished that the powerful Persian army was still in town. He could have used its help. Taxila's neighbor to the southeast, King Porus, was a brave and intelligent man who wanted Ambhi's kingdom for himself.

Still, the gossip was that the Persian army itself had fallen on hard times. Some young Greek fellow named Sikander had popped up out of nowhere—Macedonia, actually, but that was as good as nowhere—and was busily conquering the whole world. The rumor was that this Sikander character had never lost a battle. Of course, you couldn't believe everything you heard. A young boy still in his 20s couldn't possibly have conquered everything from the Nile River to Afghanistan, not to mention the mighty Persians—but still . . . the stories *might* be true.

King Ambhi's heart must have sunk when a messenger arrived with news of the horrible defeat of one of Taxila's neighbors. When the Greek Sikander and his troops had arrived in his kingdom, the neighboring king had foolishly tried to fight. But resistance had been futile. Not only had the king lost, but his city had been burned and looted. And that, the messenger would have told King Ambhi, was no

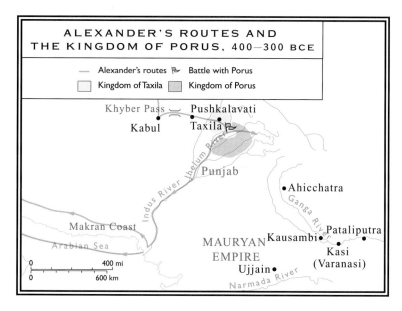

ALEXANDER'S ROUTES AND
THE KINGDOM OF PORUS, 400—300 BCE

— Alexander's routes ⚑ Battle with Porus
☐ Kingdom of Taxila ▨ Kingdom of Porus

Khyber Pass · Pushkalavati
Kabul · Taxila ⚑
Punjab
Indus River
Jhelum River
Ahicchatra ·
Ganga River
Makran Coast
Arabian Sea
MAURYAN · Kausambi · · Pataliputra
EMPIRE · Kasi
0   400 mi   Ujjain · (Varanasi)
0   600 km   Narmada River

rumor. He'd seen the terrible scene himself. Now Sikander's army was on the move again. Next stop: Taxila.

For one desperate moment, King Ambhi must have wished that he and his people could somehow jump out of Sikander's way. And then he realized that, in a way, they could.

What if he offered to help Sikander? If they were on the same side, there would be no battle. Taxila would be safe. What's more, Sikander might even help King Ambhi against his enemy King Porus.

So, when Sikander—whom you might know by his Greek name, Alexander the Great—and his army marched up to the gates of Taxila, King Ambhi was there to welcome them. Just to make sure that Alexander understood that he, King Ambhi, was a friend, he threw Alexander's army a huge party that lasted for a whole month. Arrian, a diplomat traveling with Alexander, wrote that when Alexander "arrived at Taxila, a great and flourishing city... Taxiles the governor of the city, and the Indians who belonged to it received him in a friendly manner, and he therefore added as much of the adjacent country to their territory as they requested." The present that he offered Alexander as a symbol of his good will was just as impressive: 5,000 soldiers and 56 war elephants.

❝ Arrian, *Anabasis*, second century CE

These elephants and local troops would be important to provide backup for Alexander's elite corps of around 5,000 armored cavalry (men on horseback), 14,500 archers, 5,300 regular cavalry, and around 15,000 foot soldiers. Although his troops were brave, experienced, and skillful, Alexander knew that defeating Porus would be difficult. Porus had a large army of his own—3,000 cavalry and more than 1,000 chariots, 50,000 foot soldiers and archers, and 200 war ele-

Wearing a full beard and Persian clothes, Alexander the Great meets Brahmin priests and philosophers in this Persian painting done almost 2,000 years after Alexander's death.

**FEED AN ARMY
FOR PEANUTS**

War elephants were the most valuable part of an Indian army. They typically carried several archers at once on their backs. Like modern-day tanks, they could go anywhere and were very difficult to stop. There are stories of elephants shot full of arrows who calmly removed the arrows with their own trunks. You didn't want to get in their way— if told to by their "drivers," elephants would trample anyone on foot. Elephants also frightened horses that had not been specially trained. This was particularly serious because the most powerful part of most armies was the cavalry, the soldiers who rode horseback.

phants. His soldiers were also supposed to be the tallest and most powerful warriors in Asia, with an average height of more than six feet. They looked even taller because they wore their long hair coiled on their heads and wrapped in turbans so thick that even the sharpest sword could not cut through them. They were dressed in white cotton and white leather shoes, and wore earrings set with precious stones, golden armbands, and bracelets even into battle.

At first, King Ambhi's plan seemed to have worked. Alexander marched on, leaving Taxila intact. When he got to the Jhelum River, the border between King Ambhi and Porus, Alexander demanded that Porus surrender at once. Porus, safe on the other side, refused. It was too hot to fight, and the river, rising from melting snow, was too dangerous to cross. At this time of the year, there was no grass for the army's horses and oxen, and villagers had no rice or wheat to spare for soldiers. Besides, the monsoon was expected soon, and no sensible person would try fighting during the huge rainstorms that were on their way. It was pointless. Once it started raining, everything was so muddy that horses and chariots got stuck and were useless. Only the elephants could

India's war elephants were among the most feared weapons of the ancient world. In this carving from the second century BCE, an Indian elephant crushes a Turkish soldier.

get through, and even they wouldn't be much help. The archers the elephants carried would have a hard time shooting with wet, soggy bow strings.

But Alexander had not come as far as he had to be stopped by a river or a little rain. He sent small bands of men out at night to trick Porus into thinking he was crossing the river. According to one story, Porus sent his troops to meet them, only to find out that no one was there. When Alexander and his men finally did attack, during a heavy rainstorm, the battle lasted for more than eight hours. Thousands of warriors (including both of Porus's sons) were killed or wounded, along with their horses and elephants. Porus himself was badly wounded, too. But he was just as stubborn as Alexander and, wounded or not, he led a charge against the Greeks.

By the end of the day, both armies were exhausted, and Alexander called a truce. According to a Persian poem, *Shah Nama*, written by the poet Firdausi 1,600 years later, Alexander told Porus:

> O! Noble Man:
> Our two hosts have been shattered by the fight,
> The wild beasts batten on the brains of men,
> The horses' hoofs are trampling on their bones,
> Now both of us are heroes, brave and young,
> Both **paladins** of eloquence and brain,
> Why then slaughter be the soldier's lot
> Or bare survival after combating.

Alexander's first messenger was poor unlucky King Ambhi, but Porus chased that traitor away with a spear, so Alexander sent someone else. This time, after Porus had dismounted from his horse and had a drink of water, he agreed to meet with Alexander. Although Greek historian Arrian said that Alexander won, he also said that when Alexander asked Porus how he wanted to be treated, Porus answered, "as a King." Many historians today believe that the battle ended

A godlike figure who may represent Alexander the Great holds a thunderbolt on this Greek coin. Egyptians worshipped Alexander, but he is never mentioned in texts or stories of South Asia.

❝ Firdausi, *Shah Nama*, 13th century CE

A paladin is another name for a knight. In the 13th century, poetry about paladins was as popular in Persia and Northern India as stories about King Arthur were in western Europe.

❝ Arrian, *Anabasis*, second century CE

66 Kautilya, *Arthashastra*, fourth century BCE

in a tie. Alexander granted Porus not only the land that was already his, but a good part of King Ambhi's land as well.

Although Alexander was ready to go farther, after the battle with Porus his Greek soldiers had had enough, and they refused. Their return was horrible. After fighting their way down through unfriendly Indian settlements along the Indus River to the sea, most of the army died while trying to make its way home along the treacherous and waterless Makran coast between India and Mesopotamia. Although Alexander himself got to Mesopotamia safely, he died there a few years later, when he was only 32 years old.

From an Indian point of view, the invasion of Alexander the Great was far less important than the adventures of one of King Porus's allies, a minor prince named Chandragupta. The story goes that Alexander thought that Chandragupta was not respectful enough to him and tried to have him killed, but Chandragupta ran away. By 317 BCE, the prince who ran in fear of his life would control half of the Indian subcontinent, everything from present-day Afghanistan to Bangladesh and Nepal to the central Deccan plateau— including all of the South Asian territory once held by Alexander, Porus, and Ambhi.

Chandragupta's most important weapon was not a war elephant, or even an army. It was his adviser, a clever and ambitious man named Kautilya. As a young man, Kautilya was an adviser to a king. He tried to convince the king to rule his people with knowledge and wisdom instead of by force. Kautilya claimed that "a king who observes his duty of protecting his people justly and according to law will go to heaven, whereas one who does not protect them or inflicts unjust punishment will not." The king refused and had Kautilya thrown out of his kingdom. From the gate, the king called to him, asking what good his knowledge was now.

Kautilya swore he wouldn't cut his hair until he proved that knowledge was stronger than physical force. He wrote a book that explained his ideas called the *Arthashastra*, which means "The Book of Wealth and Power." Kautilya also found a young prince who was willing to take his advice. The prince's name was Chandragupta Maurya.

Chandragupta was an excellent student. Not only did he quickly defeat Kautilya's first boss, the king who had thought knowledge was useless, but he founded the Mauryan Dynasty, India's first **centralized** government. With Kautilya's help, Chandragupta made many improvements to his empire, making it attractive to local rulers and their people.

Probably his most important improvement was building a highway system that made travel safe and even comfortable. Special guards kept an eye out for bandits. Busy and important roads were widened. According to Kautilya's *Arthashastra*, "The following roads shall be 54 feet wide: Royal Highways, roads leading to a divisional or provincial headquarters, roads in the countryside and pasture lands, roads in port towns and military quarters and roads leading a village or to a cemetery." A Greek ambassador named Megesthanes visited the court of Chandragupta and wrote that the road had stone markers at equal distances with signs at major crossroads that told travelers how far it was to the next city. By the time of Chandragupta's grandson, Ashoka, in the middle of the third century BCE, the roads were also dotted with rest stops every mile or so, complete with wells, shelters, and banyan trees for shade.

Chandragupta also established ministries, departments of officials who organized the activities that could help make his empire strong. There was a superintendent of mines, a superintendent of "ocean mines" (which regulated the trade of items from the sea, like pearls and conch shells), a superintendent of metals, and a superintendent of forests. Under the Mauryan Dynasty, citizens of the kingdom would become better fed, better educated, and wealthier than ever before—at least for a while.

In a *centralized* government, one person (or a small group) makes decisions for the whole country from the capital city. A *decentralized* government is one in which many people across the country make decisions for their own areas of responsibility.

❝ Kautilya, *Arthashastra*, fourth century BCE

This square bronze coin was among the first to be used throughout the entire Mauryan empire that didn't have to be re-stamped in each city. Engraved on these coins are traditional Indian symbols, including, on the left coin, an elephant, a sun and moon, a swastika (an ancient good luck symbol), and a banner. On the right is a hill and crescent, a bull's head, a fenced sacred tree, and a water tank in the form of a cross.

CHAPTER 17

NOTHING BUT A ZERO
SCIENCE AND TECHNOLOGY

Have you ever gone camping? People who love to camp often talk about how well they can see the stars away from city lights. They talk about noticing how early some birds wake up in the morning, and how after a few days they have figured out the best places to find lizards or wild blueberries. When you're camping, you're living close to the earth. (Some people think too close!) You have the time to see patterns that you wouldn't notice in ordinary life—like the way mint stems are square, with leaves that stick out opposite each other, and that the best time to find salamanders is after it has rained. When you go camping, you can't help noticing and wondering about the natural world. You can't help being a scientist.

The peoples of ancient India lived close to the land all the time. In a way, they were all scientists. They may not have had the tools that modern scientists do. They never learned about magnifying lenses, so they had no microscopes or telescopes. They certainly didn't have any laboratories with gleaming glassware and stainless steel sinks. But they were curious about the world in which they lived, they paid attention, and they discovered some wonderful things.

ayu + *veda* = "life" + "knowledge" or "science" *Ayurveda* means "the science of living."

The earliest and longest lasting of their discoveries are included in the traditional Indian medicine form called **Ayurveda**. Ayurveda has been around in one form or another for 5,000 years. It includes all kinds of treatments, such as herbal medicine, surgery, yoga, meditation, and massage, and teaches that disease often starts first in the mind. A lot of people still use Ayurveda. For example, many Indian mothers massage their babies with oils and apply heavy black eyeliner around their children's eyes. They believe that the massages help soothe their children and prevent stomach pains, and that the eyeliner protects their children's eyes from infections and the bright Indian sun.

Ayurvedic medicines, including herbs and essential oils, are ground into powders and prepared as teas or made into pills. Many Ayurvedic remedies are very effective and used throughout the world even today.

Some of Ayurveda's ideas are no longer popular. Most modern doctors don't treat fevers by cutting open a patient's arm or by sticking leeches—small, slimy, pond-dwelling creatures that like to suck blood—onto a patient's skin to get rid of the "sick" blood. (Although Western doctors *did* treat fevers by opening veins or using leeches until the beginning of the 20th century.)

Mostly Ayurveda was far ahead of Western medicine. Ayurvedic surgeons knew that both patients and surgical instruments had to be completely clean to stop infections during operations—something European doctors didn't figure this out until the end of the 19th century. Ayurvedic surgical instruments were made from pure steel, with blades sharp enough to split a human hair. After surgery, the surgeon sewed up the wound with fine cotton thread. Sometimes the doctor would use large ants to pinch a wound together. After the ants attached themselves to the wound, the doctor removed the ants' bodies and left the heads in place as miniature clamps.

People with long-lasting illnesses like arthritis, and rulers who wanted to stay young and strong went to special **rejuvenation** clinics. These nursing homes were probably located outside the cities, where there was less noise and pollution, and patients could rest and recover from their illnesses with daily care from doctors and nurses. Ayurveda was more than medicine. It didn't just try to make people feel better when they were sick. It taught good habits that helped people *stay* healthy.

{ From the Latin word *juvenis*, which means "young." Rejuvenation is the process of making someone or something young and fresh again.

Because Ayurvedic doctors passed down their traditions orally for thousands of years before anyone wrote them down, no one knows about the doctors and nurses who helped develop them. We *do* know a little more about South Asia's greatest scientist, a man named Aryabhata, who was born in 476 CE. As a young boy, Aryabhata loved watching the stars. Even without a telescope, Aryabhata saw a lot. He saw that the moon was light on the side that faced the sun and dark on the side that faced away. He was the first person to come up with an accurate measurement for π, a number that is used to calculate the length of curves. He realized that the earth and the other planets circled the sun, instead of the sun and the planets circling the earth. He also saw that the rising and the setting of the sun, the moon, and the stars was the result of the earth turning: "Just as a man in a boat moving forward sees the stationary objects (on either side of the river) as moving backward, just so are the stationary stars seen by the people at Lanka (i.e., on the equator) as moving exactly towards the west."

Because of what he saw and understood, he made a very accurate calendar—a great help to South Asians. All kinds of activities, from farming to religion to warfare, depended on knowing exactly what time of the year it was, or in other words, where the earth was in its yearly path around the sun.

All that is amazing enough. What is even more amazing is that a poem he wrote when he was not much more than a teenager explains all that he knew and learned without a single number, equation, or diagram. Aryabhata wanted his information to be easy to remember. So he put all the numbers into a code of letters and combinations of letters, which he explains at the beginning of the poem, called the *Aryabhatiyam*. Then, in 121 verses, he explains the way the planets move in the sky better than anyone else would for 1,000 years. For Aryabhata, astronomy was a way of understanding the gods. As he wrote, "One who knows these verses, one who knows the movements of planets and celestial spheres, goes much beyond them and attains the absolute Brahman."

At first, people learned his poem and passed it on without writing it down. The fact that it wasn't written down at

“ Aryabhata, *Aryabhatiyam*, fifth century CE

“ Aryabhata, *Aryabhatiyam*, fifth century CE

first may be one reason we still have it. Insects and mildew destroyed Indian manuscripts, which were written on birch bark or palm leaves, very quickly.

Oddly, Aryabhata seems not to have known about India's biggest contribution to math and science, although his students did. What is it? Zero. You know—nothing. Believe it or not, no one had ever considered zero a number before. Had that ever messed up their arithmetic!

If the number zero is nothing, why is it such a big deal? Because by using the number zero, people can write numbers in columns, which makes adding, subtracting, and especially multiplying and dividing much easier.

The people of ancient India, like those of ancient Rome, used a counting board to keep track of sums. A counting board had columns marked off, each standing for units of 1, 10, 100, and so on. You put pebbles or other counters in each column to stand for your number. So far, so good, you could easily record how many pebbles were in each column. But if one of the columns was empty, things got sticky. Without zero, two ones could stand for one 100 and one 1, or one 10 and one 1, or—

HOW DO YOU SPELL RELIEF?

Ayurveda is divided into eight branches:

1. Diseases of pregnancy
2. Diseases of childbirth and infancy
3. Diseases that require extraction (like thorns)
4. Diseases of the eyes, ears, and nose
5. Fevers, infections, and other internal disorders
6. Antidotes to poison
7. Psychiatry and mental health
8. Rejuvenation

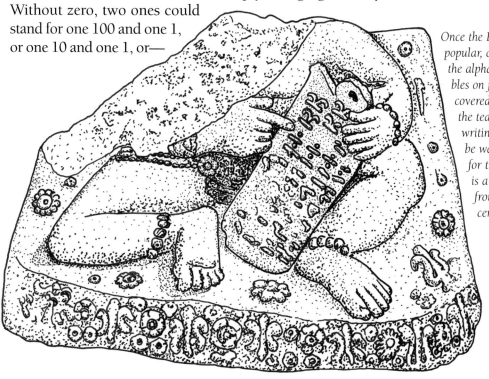

Once the Brahmi script became popular, children were taught the alphabet by writing syllables on flat wooden boards covered with white clay. After the teacher had checked their writing, the board could be washed and used again for the next lessons. This is a drawing of a figurine from the first or second century BCE.

I've Got Your Nose

People convicted of crimes in ancient India sometimes had their noses cut off as punishment. Indian surgeons came up with a kind of plastic surgery to help rebuild a sort of nose. Here is a description of how to perform the surgery:

Now I shall deal with the process of affixing an artificial nose. First the leaf of a creeper, long and broad enough to fully cover the whole of the severed or clipped off part, should be gathered, and a patch of living flesh, equal in dimension to the preceding leaf, should be sliced off (from down upward) from the region of the cheek and, after scarifying it with a knife, swiftly adhered to the severed nose. Then the cool-headed physician should steadily tie it up with a bandage... and then insert two small pipes into the nostrils to facilitate respiration.

you get the idea. Finally, someone had the bright idea of putting a small dot (which later became a circle) wherever there was an empty column. In fact, the Sanskrit word for zero is *shunya*, which means "empty."

By making arithmetic easier, the invention of zero has probably had more impact on the daily lives of people than any other scientific or technological discovery from ancient India. But if you'd asked a Mauryan emperor like Chandragupta what invention was most important to the strength of his kingdom, he probably would have told you the process of smelting iron.

Metal, especially iron, was very valuable in ancient times. Rulers used it for weapons, weights, coin manufacturing, and monuments. Iron usually starts as iron ore, a mixture of rock and metal. The iron is smelted by crushing the ore and heating it to a very high temperature. Only charcoal burned hot enough to smelt iron. India's jungles have both iron ore and lots of trees to make charcoal.

Once a blacksmith smelted the iron, he hammered it into sheets or bars that could later be shaped into swords, weights, or seals. When heating iron with charcoal, carbon fuses with the iron and makes an even harder metal called steel. Because steel is so hard, it could be used to stamp other, softer metals like gold and silver. The Mauryan government soon established mints where steel stamps called punches stamped royal symbols on pieces of silver, turning them into coins.

So many of the problems that the people of South Asia tried to solve—how to have a healthy, happy life, where we are in the universe, how to keep track of time and money—are the same problems that we try to solve today. And, despite our huge technological advantages, many of their answers continue to be help us thousands of years later. Just think what the doctors who developed Ayurveda and brilliants scientists like Aryabhata might have discovered if they'd had computers!

CHAPTER 18

DHARMA, ARTHA, KAMA, AND MOKSHA

WAR AND PEACE IN THE TIME OF ASHOKA

Prince Ashoka Maurya had two kinds of heroes. The first were the gods and goddesses of the Vedic scriptures and the prince and princesses who served them in stories such as the *Mahabharata* and the *Ramayana*. These religious heroes taught him the satisfaction of living with honor and justice (*dharma*), the excitement of money and success (*artha*), and the contentment of enjoying the world's beauties and pleasures (*kama*). They taught him that if he filled his life with these qualities of honor, excellence, and beauty, he would reach *moksha*, when the cycle of life, death, and rebirth would end.

That all sounded good to Prince Ashoka. But so did the adventures of his second kind of hero—the warrior heroes like his father, King Bindusara, and his grandfather, Chandragupta. Ashoka loved fighting, and he was good at it. He may well have gone to a military academy like the one in Taxila. Brahmins and Kshatriya came there from all over the subcontinent to learn military science, including the use of the eight major weapons. Brahmins shot bows, the Kshatriya were swordsmen, the Vaisya used the lance, and the Shudra wielded the mace—a heavy,

Emperor Ashoka erected these carved lions on top of a 45-foot (15-meter) stone pillar in 272 BCE. It celebrates the Buddha's first sermon, when he set the "wheel of law" in motion. This pillar is India's national symbol; one of the wheels under the lions' feet appears on India's flag.

Although no images of Ashoka were created during his lifetime, this drawing, made from a carving on a Buddhist stupa in South India, dates from about 100–300 CE. It shows the emperor surrounded by his female bodyguards and attendants.

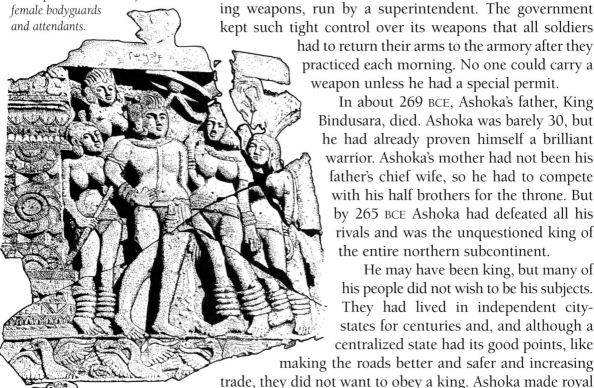

Vishakadatta, *Mudrarakshasa*, ninth century CE

spiked, hammerlike weapon. The teacher was skilled in all those weapons plus the disk (*chakra*), the spear, and fighting with his bare hands. Brahmin and Kshatriya students was also trained to command a war elephant.

Military academies like the one in Taxila show how important war was to the people of Ashoka's time. Each town had its own central armory, a strong building for storing weapons, run by a superintendent. The government kept such tight control over its weapons that all soldiers had to return their arms to the armory after they practiced each morning. No one could carry a weapon unless he had a special permit.

In about 269 BCE, Ashoka's father, King Bindusara, died. Ashoka was barely 30, but he had already proven himself a brilliant warrior. Ashoka's mother had not been his father's chief wife, so he had to compete with his half brothers for the throne. But by 265 BCE Ashoka had defeated all his rivals and was the unquestioned king of the entire northern subcontinent.

He may have been king, but many of his people did not wish to be his subjects. They had lived in independent city-states for centuries and, and although a centralized state had its good points, like making the roads better and safer and increasing trade, they did not want to obey a king. Ashoka made royal visits to these regions to persuade his people to stay in the kingdom his father and grandfather had established. When persuasion didn't work, he sent his army.

Ashoka's grandfather, Chandragupta, had united most of the northern subcontinent. His empire stretched "from the lord of the mountains [Himalayas], cooled by showers of the spray of the divine steam [Ganga] playing about among its rocks, to the shores of the southern ocean marked by the brilliance of gems flashing with various colors." Ashoka's father, Bindusara, had continued his father's tradition, earning himself the nickname "Slayer of Enemies." But neither

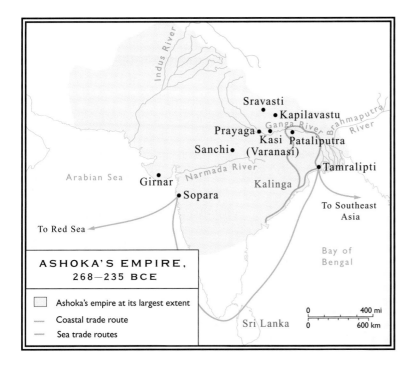

ASHOKA'S EMPIRE,
268—235 BCE

☐ Ashoka's empire at its largest extent
— Coastal trade route
— Sea trade routes

Chandragupta nor Bindusara had dared attack the territory of Kalinga in eastern India.

Kalinga was a particularly rich and powerful state. Its riches came from its trade with Southeast Asia. Merchants from Kalinga could be found as far away as Borneo, Bali, and Java. Although it had no king, Kalinga protected its riches with a huge and well-organized army, including an army of especially mighty war elephants.

Ashoka wanted Kalinga not only for its riches, but also because the highways that connected north and south India ran right through the middle of the state. And war elephants or no war elephants, what Ashoka wanted, he usually got. His attack was brutal and effective. By the time the war was over, one out of every four Kalingans was dead or wounded. Many more had been taken prisoner and were separated from what was left of their families. Those who survived faced lives as broken and barren as their wrecked houses and ruined fields. Ashoka reported that "150,000 were deported, 100,000 were killed, and many more died (from other causes)."

WAR ELEPHANTS, THE SEQUEL

Catching, training, and controlling war elephants was one of the most important skills that the military academies taught. According to Kautilya's *Arthashastra*, summer was the best time to catch a wild elephant. The best kind was about 20 years old, with "red patches, evenly fleshed, of even sides and rounded girth, with a curved backbone and well covered with flesh."

The trainer, called a *mahout*, first got the elephant used to being led around. Then he'd teach it to raise its leg to help riders climb on. Then the elephant would learn how to run, jump over obstacles, roll over, and move in formation with other elephants (moving forward, backward, zigzag, or in a circle). It would also learn how to trample and destroy horses, chariots, and men, how to fight other elephants, and how to attack forts.

❝ Ashoka, third century BCE

This column is more than 32 feet (almost 10 meters) tall and carved from a single block of sandstone. Ashoka had his stonemasons carve a message around the bottom of the column to teach his people about the Buddha.

As Ashoka stared out over the ruins left by his armies, something changed. He'd seen the agony of defeated people before, but this was different. He was different. He remembered the lessons of *dharma*, *artha*, *kama*, and *moksha*, and realized suddenly that there was nothing honorable, creative, beautiful, or peaceful about this victory.

So Ashoka, who called himself "Beloved of gods," sent out a royal edict, a message, which he had proclaimed in every village and carved into rock pillars for all to see: "After the Kalingas had been conquered, Beloved of the Gods came to feel a strong inclination towards *dharma*, a love for *dharma*, and for instruction of *dharma*. Now Beloved of the Gods feels deep remorse for having conquered the Kalingas."

Ashoka adopted a new philosophy, one he called "conquest by *dharma*," instead of by arms. As he explained in one of his proclamations:

Ashoka, third century BCE

> I have had this edict written so that sons and great-grandsons may not consider making new conquests, or that if military conquests are made, that they be done with forbearance and light punishment, or better still that they consider making conquest by *dharma* only, for that bears fruit in this world and the next. May all their intense devotion be given to this which has result in this world and the next.

He told his people that he wanted them to live in a way that would lead to an "increase of their inner worthiness." Ashoka also promoted the teachings of the Buddha and sent missionaries, including his son and his daughter, to lands as far away as Sri Lanka so that his people would not make the same mistakes he had. As he said, "All men are my children. As for my own children, I desire that they may be provided

Ashoka, third century BCE

Ashoka, third century BCE

Ashoka, third century BCE

with all the welfare and happiness of this world and of the next, so do I desire for all men as well."

As part of his reforms, Ashoka banned the sacrifice of animals. This confused and angered many of his people, especially the Brahmins who made their living by performing animal sacrifices. The Brahmins were powerful enemies, and convinced the leaders of one region after another to break away from the Mauryan Empire after Ashoka's death. The last Mauryan ruler was assassinated in 185 BCE by one of his generals—who was, not so coincidentally, a Brahmin. Although other kings would follow, no ruler would be strong enough to unite the many different people of the subcontinent into a single political state for 1,600 years.

AND YOU THOUGHT YOUR HANDWRITING WAS BAD

The people living under Ashoka's rule spoke many different languages, so scribes needed to write his edicts, or messages, in all kinds of languages. One particularly popular way of communicating was a carved stone pillar, which would last a long time. Scholars think that first a Brahmin scribe probably copied the inscriptions with a piece of charcoal and then a craftsman carved them. The craftsmen, some of whom could not read, were sometimes sloppy, and this makes it difficult for scholars to figure out some of the letters.

This spectacular temple at Bodh Gaya, India, marks the place where the Buddha sat under a bodhi, or banyan, tree and gained enlightenment. The original temple was built by Ashoka, but it has been rebuilt and expanded many times during the past 2,000 years.

CHAPTER 19

**❝ ILANGO ADIGAL
AND THE VEDAS**

SERVICE AND STUDY
THE CYCLE OF LIFE

❝ Ilango Adigal, "The Ankle
Bracelet," about 200 BCE–
200 CE

Sometime between 200 BCE and 200 CE, a Jain author named Ilango Adigal wrote a story called "The Ankle Bracelet." "The Ankle Bracelet" tells the tale of a married couple, Kannaki and her foolish husband Kovalan. After Kovalan wastes all their money, they decide to move and begin a new life. The journey is long and difficult, and they are very glad to arrive at the house of some poor cowherds: "Madari the cowherdess had joyfully taken charge of the frail Kannaki. In the sheltered cottage to which she led her, cowgirls lived who wore shining bracelets. Thorny hedges kept it private from other huts inhabited by the cowherds who sold buttermilk."

The beginning of a boy's formal education was marked by a ceremony observed by his family and friends. Mothers taught girls household rituals and duties in preparation for their eventual marriage, when they would run the household.

The ancient people of South Asia believed that unmarried women should be protected from men. Although the cowgirls are so poor that they must go out to work (and so poor that their jewelry is made out of Indian rosewood instead of gold), they are still guarded by the thorn bushes. Turning toward the girls, Madari says, "Her master observes all the rules of the pious Jains, who do not eat after sunset. Bring at once our best saucepans so that Kannaki may help Aiyai to prepare a good meal." The cowgirls bring new utensils, as is done for wealthy people. There are also white-striped cucumbers, green pomegranates and mangoes, sweet bananas, good rice, and fresh cow's milk.

Members of the Jain religion are very careful not to hurt or kill any other living creature. They don't eat after sunset so that they won't accidentally swallow insects attracted by lamps. They are also vegetarians. After Kannaki prepares the meal,

66 Ilango Adigal, "The Ankle Bracelet," about 200 BCE–200 CE

> Kovalan seated himself on a small expertly woven palm-leaf mat. Then Kannaki, with her flower-hands, poured water from a jug to wash her master's feet. As if attempting to awaken our mother Earth from a swoon, she sprinkled water on the ground and beat the soil with her palms. Then she placed before her husband a tender plantain leaf and said, "Here is your food, my lord. May you be pleased to eat." Having performed with care the rites prescribed for the sons of merchants, they ate their dinner together.

66 Ilango Adigal, "The Ankle Bracelet," about 200 BCE–200 CE

Kannaki performs several rituals as she serves her husband dinner. When Kannaki washes her husband's feet, she shows her respect and love for him. Ancient carvings show other ways that people displayed respect: someone touching another's feet or the ground near the feet, touching a seated person's knee, or

This terracotta figurine of a person with hands clasped in greetings or prayer was made at Harappa about 4,500 years ago. This same gesture is still used throughout South Asia today.

A young bride has placed a streak of red vermilion in the part of her hair to indicate her married status. The gold necklaces and bangles are her insurance against hard times.

Ilango Adigal, "The Ankle Bracelet," about 200 BCE–200 CE

putting both hands together and, while holding them in front of the face, bowing the head. (It was always improper to touch anyone from a different caste, though.)

Before serving dinner, Kannaki also sanctifies, or makes sacred, the eating place. To do this, she sprinkles water to settle the dust and then plasters with mud the spot where her husband will eat. In many strict Brahmin homes, food can be served only on a freshly plastered floor that has been purified with a thin coating of clay and manure from a sacred cow. Because their hosts are poor, Kovalan sits on the ground and eats off a banana-leaf plate. Unless invited to join their husbands, women eat in the kitchens after their husbands are finished. In the story of Kannaki and Kovolan, they eat together because they are deeply in love.

After dinner, Kannaki gives her husband one of her ankle bracelets to sell in the city to get money for them to start a new life. It's a big sacrifice—a woman's jewelry is given to her when she marries and is almost never sold. It would be like a woman from modern Western culture giving her husband her engagement and wedding rings to sell. In the unlucky story of Kovalan, he takes the ankle bracelet to an evil goldsmith, who kills him and steals the bracelet.

Although Kovalan wasted all their money, Kannaki loved him and mourned him as a good wife should. She breaks all her bracelets, climbs a sacred mountain, and vows not to rest until she is with him again:

> For 14 days she lay there until the king of the heavens [Indra] with all of his angels finally decided to proclaim the saintliness of this woman. He showered her with flowers and then appeared and bowed at her feet. In the end he took her to heaven in a chariot as a goddess and seated beside her was her husband Kovalan. The god sings,

> "Even the gods pay honor to the wife
> who worships no one save her husband,
> Kannaki, pearl among all women of the earth,
> Is now a goddess, and is highly honored
> By all the gods who dwell in paradise."

Although it sometimes may seem that most South Asian history is about men, stories like the "The Ankle Bracelet" tell us that the women who cared for their families were also doing honorable and important work.

While the lives of women in ancient India revolved around caring for their husbands and families, a man's life was divided into four stages: student, parent, hermit, and renouncer. The life of a student began early—mothers "taught" their babies even before they were born by praying, fasting, and singing praises to the gods. Young children stayed home and played with other boys and girls until they were ready for school. Brahmin boys started school at age 8, while Kshatriya and Vaisya boys had to wait until they were 10 or 12 years old. Shudras did not study at all.

If you were a boy from one of the three upper classes, you went through a special initiation ceremony when you started school that celebrated your "rebirth" as a student of the Vedic scriptures. During the ceremony, you would be given an unsewn two-piece robe that wrapped around your waist and draped over your shoulders (somehow meant to keep you from forgetting what you were about to learn), a belt, a staff, and a sacred thread to wear over your left shoulder. The study of the Vedas was a very serious thing. If a boy didn't want to study the Vedas, he was cut off from his community. The Vedas taught that people should treat boys who refused to study this way: "One shall not initiate them, one shall not teach them, one shall not associate with them in sacrifices and one shall not have social dealings with them."

From about 1500 to 500 BCE, girls could also be initiated into the study of the Vedas and had the right to wear the sacred thread and belt. One Veda says, "A young daughter who has finished her studies should be married to a bridegroom who like her is learned." Women also composed some of the Vedic hymns. But over time people came to believe that a woman's real initiation took place when she became a wife and a mother.

Students didn't study the Vedas in a classroom with all their friends. Instead, their teachers gave each student specific lessons. As soon as the student mastered the lesson, he

SATI—SAD BUT TRUE

According to early Vedic tradition, when a man died, his wife would lie beside him on the funeral pyre and symbolically join him in the afterlife. But she left before the fire started burning, and she was allowed to remarry. Later, women began to be burned alive with their husbands. Scholars believe that this practice began during the sixth century BCE, a time of war and invasions when women left alone were not safe. The women who chose to die with their husbands believed that their sins were burned away and that they would become part of the goddess Sati, the wife of Shiva. The women were called *sati*, which means "true, good, virtuous."

❝ Brahmanical Code of Conduct, 600–100 BCE

❝ Yajurveda, 800–700 BCE

Code of Manu, 200–300 CE

could go on. Most students studied for about 12 years, although it could take longer if the student had a hard time memorizing the basic Vedas. Teachers were supposed to be strict but kind: "The good of creatures should be effected with kind sympathetic means; desiring virtue, one shall use sweet and gentle words under the circumstances."

Students could go to universities in Taxila and other places after they graduated from their first teacher, or they could find another teacher to tutor them. But most young men got married and began a family. Wealthy men like King Ashoka could marry more than one woman, but usually only one woman was the chief wife. Each community and class had different wedding ceremonies, but they all involved the man and woman purifying (cleaning) themselves and then walking around the sacred fire. After marriage, women wore special jewelry. The kind of jewelry she wore depended on her class and where she lived, but it often included hair ornaments, earrings, bangles, bracelets, and a pendant necklace called a *mangal sutra*. Married women also marked the parts of their hair with the sacred color red, which meant blood, life, fertility, and power.

The third stage of a man's life began when his hair turned white. At that point, he was supposed to give his wealth to his oldest son and retire. He'd join a community of elderly men living in the forest, and spend his day teaching a new generation of boys, meditating, and practicing yoga. Older women would either stay with their son's family or become nuns.

After the birth of his first grandson, a man reached the fourth stage of his life—renunciation. At this stage, the grandfather left his family and became a wandering beggar. Sometimes he'd travel with friends. When he became too old to travel,

People who had given away all their wealth could go to monasteries or shrines to meditate and live a life of worship. This yaksha, or "earth spirit," guards the walkway around the Buddhist shrine at Barhut, India.

he'd stay at a temple, living off whatever people gave him until he died and was reborn in a new cycle of life. After his death, his oldest son performed a funeral ceremony, offering water and small balls of rice to feed his father's spirit on his way to the world of the ancestors. When a son does this for his father today, he puts a clay pot filled with water on his shoulder. He breaks a hole in the pot and walks around his father's funeral pyre until the water is all gone. Then he breaks the pot, marking the end of his father's time on earth.

Although some of the early Vedic communities buried their dead, in time they switched to burning the bodies. They believed that this practice, called cremation, returned the body to the five basic elements of earth, water, air, fire, and space. Family members would then scatter the remaining ashes in the water of a river that would flow to the sea and then became joined with the sacred Ganga River.

Many elderly people move to the sacred city of Varanasi, India, so that they can die and be cremated along the banks of the Ganga River. Worshippers attend a cremation and will throw the ashes into the river.

CHAPTER 20

" KUSHANA COIN,
STUPA, AND
BUDDHIST CAVE
IN INDIA

WHO'S IN CHARGE HERE, ANYWAY?

AN AGE OF RELIGIOUS AND POLITICAL CONFUSION

After the death of Ashoka in 232 BCE, no one ruler was strong enough to control all of South Asia. Historians call that a "power vacuum," and it is a dangerous time to be alive. When no one is control, leaders fight each other instead of caring for the people.

For a while, the Bactrian Greeks from the highlands of Central Asia seemed to be the winners of South Asia's power struggle. Originally ruled by Greek generals whom Alexander the Great had left behind, the Bactrian Greeks eventually broke away from Alexander's empire. Then the Parthians, horsemen from the plains of present-day Iran, attacked South Asia, followed by the Scythians, people from the high plains of Central Asia. Meanwhile, princes in south and central India battled each other for land and power.

Bactria
Purushapura• •Taxila
(Peshawar)
Parthia

CHINA

Indus River

Himalayas

Mathura•
Ganga River

Kasi •Pataliputra
(Varanasi) Bihar

Arabian Sea
Narmada River

Bay of Bengal

**KUSHANA EMPIRE UNDER
KANISHKA, 120—143 CE**

☐ Kushana Empire at its largest extent
▨ Areas allied with Kushana Empire

0   400 mi
0   600 km

Like a bunch of rowdy kids, the Parthians and the Bactrian Greeks fought each other, and both waged war against Indo-Greek and local rulers in the northern Indus Valley. Local kings and princes squabbled with each other and punched the Parthians while no one else was looking. Without a strong emperor keeping an eye on things, ambitious leaders all hoped that, with a little luck and a lot of bravery, they could unite the continent and become the next Ashoka.

Even if they no longer shared the same government, many people living in the subcontinent shared religious beliefs, beliefs that turned into today's Hinduism. They prayed to gods such as Vishnu, Brahma, and Shiva. They believed that people were born into one of four *varnas*, or classes, according to the way they had lived in their previous lives. They hoped that by carefully following the rules of their *varna*, they would achieve *moksha*, or release from the cycle of rebirth, and unite with the universe.

Many of these people also loved and admired the Buddha and followed his teachings. Many learned about the Buddha from monuments and missionaries of Emperor Ashoka. But following the Buddha was tricky. The Buddha was not a god and did not claim to be. And there were no rules or system—no religion—that explained how to become like him.

During the more than 400 years since his death, the Buddha had been remembered and honored only by burial mounds called stupas, built to hold tiny containers of ashes from his cremated body. At these holy places, people built monuments like the stone columns that Ashoka raised.

A princely bodhisattva holds a lotus, which represents the teachings of the Buddha. Bodhisattvas usually shown as wealthy princes, complete with fancy headdresses and jewelry, were people who were worthy of achieving nirvana, but voluntarily held back so that they could help others.

**MEANWHILE
IN CHINA...**

During the time of Ashoka, China was divided by civil wars. They were ended in 221 BCE by a remarkable man from the western province of Qin, who called himself Qin Shi Huangdi. *Shi Huangdi* is usually translated as "The First Emperor," but another one of its meanings is "First Dread Lord," and it fits. During the 15 years of his reign, he brought together the huge empire of China and gave his name to it, built part of the Great Wall of China, made standard rules for Chinese writing, law, currency, weights and measures, and built large palaces and forts. He also burned all books written during the reigns of earlier emperors, and punished scholars who didn't like the book burning by burying them alive. The Kushana tribes probably moved west into Bactria to get out of his way.

The sculptor of this panel carved images of the same man and woman to the left, behind, and to the right of a dome-shaped stupa. Buddhists walked around the stupa and touched it to help them feel closer to the Buddha.

These columns were decorated with symbols of the Buddha's life, such as an empty foot cushion or a footprint to show that he had been there, but not pictures of the Buddha himself.

But during the upset of the centuries before and after 1 CE, people wanted more than just monuments and the example of Buddha's life to follow. Times were hard. Life was uncertain. And the rulers in charge kept changing. In the confusion of new leaders (some of whom spoke new languages) and constant war, ordinary men and women wanted something that they could hold onto, something that would last. They wanted rules with guaranteed results. At one time, the religion of the Brahmins gave that. If you wanted something from a god, you paid a Brahmin priest to make a sacrifice for you. But now—well, the Buddha had said that all violence was bad, including killing sacrificial animals. And there had been so much blood already.

During the second century BCE, a tribe called the Kushana moved from Central Asia into what is now northern Afghanistan. At first, their arrival seemed like one more unwelcome bit of confusion. The Kushana were central Asian people with ties to China, with whom they traded. Once settled in their new home, the Kushana set about learning Greek philosophy and culture from the Bactrian Greeks, Persian religion and culture from the Parthians, and Buddhist and early Hindu teachings from the Indians. And, unlikely though it sounds, it was their great leader Kanishka, an outsider from Central Asia, who united the peoples of South Asia.

We don't know much about his personal life, but we know Kanishka loved trying out new things. Because the Romans were the richest and most powerful people in the West, he modeled the weight and value of his gold and silver coins after their coins and that of their Greek allies. Even the names of the coins came from the Romans and Greeks: Kushana gold coins were called *dinara*, after the Latin *denarius*, and the silver coins were called *dramma*, after the Greek *drachma*.

The designs of the coins are another example of Kanishka's love of different ideas. Like many other coins, Kanishka's have a picture of him on one side, and many have the words "King of Kings Kanishka Kushana." But the second side was different. It shows gods and leaders from many different religions—everyone from Shiva and the Greek gods Hephaestus and Helios to the Persian goddess of fortune. Some of Kanishka's coins have what may be the first images of the Buddha.

Kanishka was willing to listen to any religion, and to let his people worship whomever and however they wished. This was unusual in a ruler. The great emperor Ashoka had been tolerant, but he was also unusual. Kanishka was similar to Ashoka in many ways. Both Kanishka and Ashoka were

FIND THE BUDDHA

Although there were no images of the Buddha until about Year 1, his followers used symbols of the four stages of his life to remind them of him. A lotus blossom was the symbol of his miraculous birth. The pipal tree—the kind of tree that shaded him at the moment of his enlightenment—was the symbol of his enlightenment. A wheel represents his first sermon (the wheel stands for the Wheel of Law that the Buddha set in motion). The stupas themselves symbolize his death.

66 Kanishka Kushana coin, second century CE

This coin shows the ruler Kanishka (top) on one side and the Indo-Iranian deity Miiro or Mithras on the other (left). In the Vedas, this deity was called Mitra.

66 Stupa, third century BCE, Sanchi, India

Buddhists believed that the umbrella-shaped object at the top of stupas represented the place where eternity and earthly life came together. Worshipers could only climb there spiritually.

bodhi + *sattva* = "perfect knowledge" + "being or reality" A *bodhisattva* is a being of perfect knowledge who unselfishly and lovingly helps others to become like him.

ambitious rulers who loved fighting and conquest and also loved learning about new things and trying them on for size. Like Ashoka, Kanishka learned about the gentle religion of Buddhism. And like Ashoka, Kanishka wanted to share it with his people.

Ashoka sent missionaries and built stupas and stone monuments in order to spread Buddha's message—which was a good start. But Kanishka looked around at early Hindu temples to Vishnu and Krishna, and he wanted to do more for Buddhism. By about 200 CE, Buddhist temples had become more elaborate. Built out of stone now instead of wood, they were decorated with stone and terracotta, or baked red clay, images of the gods and goddesses. Ordinary worshippers could see the gods they admired and they could make sacrifices to them right there. What if Buddhists could do the same thing?

Kanishka called a huge meeting of Buddhists. During the council, important Buddhist monks said that the old ways of teaching Buddhism were fine if you were an educated, disciplined person without the responsibility of a family, but that they weren't inspiring enough for most ordinary Indians. Ordinary people wanted statues and paintings of the Buddha that could help them feel more connected to him. They needed saints, called **bodhisattvas,** holy figures who were not quite as awesome as the Buddha, who might be willing to help sinners like themselves. And they liked to worship together with their neighbors and the people they loved, whether by singing the same songs, dancing the same dances, or celebrating festivals together.

The monks made reforms known as "Mahayana" Buddhism. Statues, festivals, saints, temples, and rituals drew more people to the Buddhist path. Some Buddhists liked things the old way—this group was called Theravada Buddhists, which means those Buddhists who followed the original "teachings of the elders."

Kanishka was like Ashoka in another way. His well-organized empire grew quickly and grew wealthy from trading with all the different people he had worked so hard to include—the people of China, Rome, Iran, and many regions of South Asia itself. But, like Ashoka's empire, it did not last. By the end of the third century BCE, ambitious local rulers had begun to overpower Kushana officials.

In the end, Kanishka's empire was short-lived, but today, his great Buddhist sites dot all of South Asia—from Afghanistan, Pakistan, and Bangladesh to Tibet, Nepal, and Sri Lanka. Many of the sites are caves with images of the Buddha carved and painted right on the rock walls. Buddhist monks, more numerous after Kanishka's great council, took care of the caves. And while armies fought, merchants quietly began to use these caves as beautiful banks, safe places to leave their riches. Today, along with Ashoka's stupas, they are among South Asia's greatest cultural treasures.

Buddhist cave, second century BCE, Ajanta, India

This carving of the Buddha meditating at a cave in Ajanta provided inspiration for monks and pilgrims.

CHAPTER 21

A PLACE FOR EVERYONE
CASTE AND SOCIETY

For centuries, the people of South Asia had been able to tell a lot about each other with a single glance. Men in white with a thread over their left shoulders were the "twice-born" Brahmins who did the thinking for everyone. Men in blood red, with or without the sacred thread, were the Kshatriya, the warriors and kings who did the fighting for everyone. Men in yellow were the Vaisya, the merchants who made wealth for everyone. And men in black were the Shudra, the workers who served everyone.

But by 1 CE, this well-organized society was beginning to fall apart. How were you supposed to treat a Kushana? Or a Bactrian Greek? Or a Parthian? Not to mention the people from Arabia, Egypt, Ethiopia, the Mediterranean, Central Asia, Southeast Asia, or China? And what were you supposed to do when you had a ruler like Kanishka or Ashoka who supported all kinds of religions? It was all turning into one big confusing mess. New languages, new gods, new ways of doing things—no wonder everyone was fighting all the time. How can you avoid misunderstanding and conflict if people don't understand their place in society?

Some people thought that what South Asia needed was some good, old-fashioned rules. Rules were something that everyone knew and understood. And the Brahmins were just the ones to make them.

In the first century CE, the Brahmins began to refer to a text called the **Code of Manu**. It was supposed to be a record of the laws that the Creator, Brahma, gave to the first man, whose name was—you guessed it—Manu. These laws were supposed to explain your *dharma* to you—your duty, your purpose, your special calling in the world. How did you know what you were supposed to be when you grow up? How did you decide the best way to use your time? How should you treat your friend? The Code of Manu said

Manu = "man"
Manu is the Sanskrit word for "man." The Code of Manu was the law of men and women that told them how they ought to behave with each other.

This scene of palace life painted on a cave wall shows the diversity of classes and castes during the Gupta period. Elegantly dressed royalty sit next to simply clothed monks and Brahmins.

that the answer was simple. "The root of dharma is the entire Veda, and the tradition and practice of those who know the Veda." In other words, pay attention to the Vedas, the ancient sacred hymns that the Brahmins considered a handbook to life.

The Code of Manu was very clear that the *varna* you belonged to decided a whole lot about your life. It said that Shudras existed only to serve the other three *varnas*. That didn't mean that the Shudras weren't important. They were. Society needed everyone. It's just that it needed some of those people to be servants. The Code of Manu also subdivided the four major *varnas* into a number of subgroups, called *castes*, that were based on the kind of work each family did. For example, gold workers and traders were both Vaisyas, but belonged to different castes.

The Code of Manu made it clear that people who were born into a caste should only marry people from the same caste and that they should not try to change their caste or move up in society. It also said some things about women that are hard for 21st-century readers to understand:

66 Code of Manu, 200–300 CE

THAT'S A WRAP

The Code of Manu's rules and regulations for each caste were strict. For example, Brahmin clothing was supposed to be wrapped, not stitched. Stitched clothing was considered a foreign style, and could not be worn by anyone performing a ritual.

❝ Code of Manu, 200–300 CE

Even in her own home, a female—whether she is a child, a young woman, or an old lady—should never carry out any task independently. As a child, she must remain under her father's control; as a young woman, under her husband's and even when her husband is dead, under her sons'. She must never seek to live independently. She must never want to separate herself from her father, husband or sons; for by separating herself from them, a woman brings disgrace on both families. She should be always cheerful, clever at housework, careful in keeping the utensils clean and frugal in her expenditure.

This did not mean that the Brahmins who made up the Code of Manu thought women were not smart or unimpor-

This scene from the Ramayana *depicts the gods (above) who were born as monkeys (below) with supernatural powers to help Rama rescue Sita from the evil demon Ravana.*

tant, though. They just believed that in a well-ordered society, women did their most important work at home, taking care of their families. The code claims that "On account of offspring, a wife is the bearer of many blessings, worthy of honor, and the light within a home; indeed in a home no distinction at all exists between a wife and Sri, the Goddess of Fortune."

How did all these differences begin? Did Brahma make the people he liked Brahmins and the ones he didn't Shudras? Not at all. According to the sacred poem the *Mahabharata*, the "world, as created by Brahma, which was at first entirely Brahmanical, has become divided into classes, in consequence of men's actions." In other words, if you were born a Shudra, it was no one's fault but your own. You'd made a lot of mistakes in your last life resulting in bad *karma*, and now you had to pay your dues.

The upside was that if doing something bad could get you in trouble, doing something good could fix it. If you changed your behavior, your good *karma* meant that your next life would be a better one. A big part of making your next life a good one was following the rules of the life you were in.

Many of those rules meant keeping yourself clean—in a spiritual way. Dirt can't pollute you spiritually, but touching something that is not right for your caste will. Brahmins were allowed to make animal sacrifices, and sometimes they even ate meat, but they did this as part of their sacred rituals. If you did not follow the actions, or rituals, of your caste, you became ritually unclean. A leather worker, on the other hand, spent all day with the skins of dead animals, covered with flies and blood. His work made him both dirty and ritually polluted. Because leather could not be made pure by fire,

❝ Code of Manu, 200–300 CE

❝ *Mahabharata*, 400 BCE–400 CE

HOW AM I SUPPOSED TO DO IT IF I'M DEAD?

The death of your body made your spirit "unclean." The only way to make yourself pure was to be cremated, by one of your sons if possible.

According to the Code of Manu, if a man did not have a son, he could name one of his daughters a "female-son" so she could do the ritual for him.

A Brahmin priest wears the sacred thread and two pieces of unstitched clothing. One piece of cloth is wrapped around his waist and the other is draped over his left shoulder.

Brahmins were not allowed to use leather, even for their shoes. Instead, they wore wooden clogs that had string straps or a small knob sticking out of the top of the sole that they stuck between their toes. They could walk and run in these clogs, but they made lot of noise. This clack, clack, clack was an important signal for people of other castes. It meant that a Brahmin was coming and they should move out of the way so that they didn't touch him.

If you became ritually polluted, there were ways to "clean" yourself according to your caste. The Code of Manu says that:

Code of Manu, 200–300 CE

A man who desires bodily purification should first sip water three times and then wipe the mouth with water twice; but a woman or Shudra sips and wipes just once. Shudras who abide by the proper mode of conduct should shave their heads once a month, follow the rules of purification laid down for Vaisyas, and eat the leftover food of twice-born persons.

These antique clogs carved with intricate decorations are from Chitral, Pakistan, where the Kalasha people still practice many of the ancient Vedic and Brahmanical traditions.

From today's point of view, the Code of Manu seems unfair, even cruel. Although the modern governments of South Asia have banned the caste system, some communities still use many parts of the laws of Manu to keep order, just as they did more than 2,000 years ago.

CHAPTER 22

SOUTH ASIA'S GOLDEN AGE
THE GUPTA EMPIRE

In about 320 CE, a minor Indian prince married an Indian princess. In a region with more than 30 kingdoms and states, one more royal marriage wouldn't seem to be a big deal—but this one was. The prince, whose name was Chandra, came from one of India's smaller kingdoms. (Although his family name was Gupta, he probably wasn't related to the Mauryan emperor, Chandragupta.) His young wife came from the Licchavi family, who controlled what is now northeastern India and Nepal. Their marriage, and Chandra Gupta's conquests, brought together northern and central India for the first time since soon after Ashoka's death, more than 500 years before—a *very* big deal.

We don't know a whole lot about Chandra Gupta I, who ruled for only 15 years—only what historians have pieced together from coins, inscriptions, and archaeological evidence. His reign was probably a bumpy one, because his son, Samudra Gupta, had to recapture territory once controlled by his father.

We know more about Samudra Gupta, who wanted it that way. One of the stone columns Ashoka had put up 500

The gold coin on the left shows Samudra Gupta playing a stringed instrument called a vina, which represents his artistic achievements. The coin on the right depicts his grandson Kumara Gupta on a war elephant.

WHO YOU GONNA CALL?

Nicknames were important in Gupta times. Chandra Gupta II, Samudra Gupta's son, was known as "Universal Lord," "Moon Among Kings," "the Sun of Valor," "Valorous like a Lion" (when he conquered Gujarat, the land of the lions), and "Conquerer of Tigers" (when he conquered Bengal, land of the tigers). But Samudra Gupta's nicknames were the best. The "King of Poets," was also called "Uprooter of Kings," and, even more spectacularly, "Sadhvasad-hudayapralayahetupursasy-acintyasya," which means "A hero unfathomable, the cause of the elevation of the good and the destruction of the bad, and thus a counterpart of the Unfathomable Absolute, which is the cause of the creation and destruction of the world, and in which the good and the bad have their being."

Where's the beef?

Fa Hien was a Chinese Buddhist pilgrim who visited central India at the beginning of the fifth century CE. *He wrote that:*

Throughout the whole country the people do not kill any living creature, nor drink intoxicating liquor, nor eat onions or garlic. The only exception is that of the Chandalas. In that country they do not keep pigs and fowls and do not sell live cattle; in the markets there are no butcher's shops and no dealers in intoxicating drink.

Kalidasa, *Malavikagnimitram,* fourth century CE

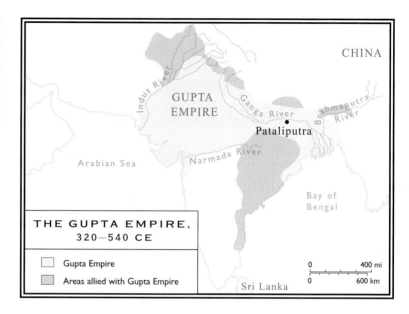

THE GUPTA EMPIRE, 320—540 CE

Gupta Empire

Areas allied with Gupta Empire

years earlier had a short inscription on it about peace. Samudra Gupta noticed that there was still a lot of perfectly good blank space on the column, so he had one of his ministers add a long description of all the battles he won and what a wonderful king he was. Samudra Gupta's nickname was "King of Poets." The Gupta court even had poet-announcers whose job it was to sing the praises of the king. They also announced the time for the king's bath and meals by loudly singing songs such as this one, which called him to lunch:

Victory to the king! The sun has climbed up to the zenith, for the geese rest with closed eyes in the shade of the leaves of the lotuses on the ornamental water, the pigeons shun on account of the extreme heat the sloping roofs of the palace which they ordinarily frequent, the peacocks desirous of drinking the particles of water continually flung out, fly to the revolving water-wheel, the sun blazes with all his rays at once, as thou with all thy princely qualities.

Besides conquering new land and making sure that everyone knew what a terrific, wise, and sensitive king he was, Samudra Gupta tried out a new form of government.

According to Kautilya's *Arthashastra*, kings had total power. But Samudra Gupta thought that his people might be happier in his kingdom if he let local leaders make some of the decisions. These local lords were called **Maharajas**. Letting the Maharajas do some of the governing proved to be a very popular decision.

In 376 CE Samudra Gupta's son, Rama Gupta, succeeded him. Even though he was named after the hero of the *Ramayana*, Rama Gupta was a coward. When he became surrounded during a battle, Rama Gupta made a deal that he'd give his wife to his enemies if they let him go free. When Rama Gupta's little brother, Chandra Gupta II, heard about what had happened, he was furious. And he had a

maha + raja =
"great" + "king"
South Asia was so big and transportation and communication were so difficult that Maharajas often did most of the governing.

This cave painting depicts a story about a prince and princess who, having been banished from their kingdom, pass through the royal gardens with their attendants.

❝ Visakhadatta, *Devi-Chandraguptam*, fourth century CE

DOES ANYBODY HAVE THE TIME?

A water clock kept time in the Gupta court. Used since Mauryan times, the water clock was a large copper vessel with a thin, delicate copper bowl floating inside. In the bottom of the bowl was a small pinhole that let the water spring up.

Young boys were in charge of the water clock. One would beat a drum to signal the time and the other would empty and float the bowl each time it filled with water. In the morning, one stroke of the drum meant that the boy put the bowl in the copper vessel. The bowl filled with water, then was emptied, filled, and emptied four times—that was one "hour." There were two "hours" in the morning until noon, and two "hours" in the afternoon. The whole day was divided into eight "hours."

plan. He dressed up as his brother's queen, and his warriors dressed up as her ladies-in-waiting. One nervous soldier wasn't so sure about the plan. He pointed out that even if they infiltrated the enemy, they would be badly outnumbered. Chandra Gupta II answered him this way: "The animals of the forest, though in a pack, at the very scent of a lonely lion, who has unfurled the cluster of his mane, run in fear. For a heroic person, number is immaterial."

The trick worked. When the enemy king got close to the "queen," Chandra Gupta II pulled out his weapons and killed him and then took control of the palace. He then became king and married his brother's wife.

Chandra Gupta II was a very good king, who believed his duty (*dharma*) was to make peace and wealth for his people. Like his father, he shared his power with local leaders, but just in case they disagreed with him, he also built a lot of forts to help defend his conquests. He believed that part of his duty was to bring order to society, which he did by reemphasizing the four castes. Before his reign, people from different varna, or classes, and castes had sometimes married each other (his own grandparents were from different classes), and people sometimes changed their line of work. Now those changes became more difficult.

Gupta society included a caste called the Chandalas, who were even lower than the Shudras. Their job was to carry the corpses to the cremation grounds outside the city and execute the worst kinds of criminals. Unlike vegetarian Brahmins, they fished, hunted, and ate meat. Because they touched dead bodies so often, they were ritually polluted and were not allowed to live inside town limits. They lived outside the town walls, beyond the place where they carried dead bodies to be burned. The Chandalas were called the Untouchables. When they came into towns on business, they clapped two pieces of wood so that everyone would know to move out of the way to avoid touching them.

Besides strengthening Brahmin ideas about caste, the Gupta rulers also worshipped early Hindu gods. They used a symbol, the eagle Garuda who carried Vishnu, the god of preservation, as their royal insignia. By this time, Brahmins did not make many animal sacrifices, they made offerings of milk and grain to avatars of Vishnu like Krishna and Vamana, the Dwarf. The mother goddess, who was the partner of both Vishnu and Shiva, also became very popular.

Even though the Guptas followed Brahmin ways, they also supported Buddhist and Jain schools and temples. A Buddhist pilgrim from China named Xuanzang wrote that the king "would provide choice meats for men of all sorts of religion." No matter what the dietary rules of your religion, the royal kitchens made sure that you had something to eat.

> Xuanzang, *A Record of the Western Regions*, seventh century CE

The Guptas were excellent rulers, but even they could not stop what happened next. In the middle of the fifth century CE, tribes of White Huns, a nomad people from Central Asia, began raiding northern India, burning and robbing monasteries, temples, and towns on their way. A Gupta king named Skanda Gupta managed to defeat them. One royal order described the fight this way: "by his two arms shook the earth, when he joined in close conflict with the Huns."

> Pillar inscription, Bhitari, India, fifth century CE

But this did not stop the destruction by the Huns. The Maharajas who once served the Gupta kings were busy defending their own people, and the Gupta Empire fell apart. In time, the Huns settled down and married local Kshatriya rulers. These Maharajas adopted local customs, clothing styles, and even religious beliefs, adding one more layer of diversity to the ever-changing cultures of South Asia.

CHAPTER 23

XUANZANG AND BHAGAVATA PURAN

GODS AND CAVES
LITERATURE AND ART OF THE GUPTA ERA

Xuanzang, *A Record of the Western Regions*, seventh century CE

In 627 CE, a 25-year-old Buddhist monk found himself looking out over the dunes of the River of Sand, where "there is neither bird nor animal nor water nor grazing." The only things he could see under the burning white sun and endless blue sky were the sand, his red horse, and his own tall shadow. The monk's name was Xuanzang, and what he was doing—crossing the barren desert that lay between China and India—was against the law.

Turkish people related to the White Huns who had caused such trouble for the Kushana were attacking China's western border, and the Chinese emperor had banned all foreign travel. But Xuanzang was determined to see the places where the Buddha had walked and to find good, clear records of the Buddha's teachings. The only translations he could find in China were terrible. Xuanzang wrote that "the sounds of the words translated were often mistaken . . . and the sense of the books was lost." They were so awful, in fact, that they could drive a monk to—well, to cross a desolate desert against the orders of his emperor.

Xuanzang, *A Record of the Western Regions*, seventh century CE

It took Xuanzang more than a year to complete his long and lonely journey along the Great Silk Road to India, the overland route west from China. So perhaps it isn't surprising that once he had arrived, he stayed for 13 years, visiting Buddhist scholars and tourist sites and gathering Buddhist writings to take home with him.

He probably would have said that the most important part of his trip was the years he spent at the University of Nalanda. Ashoka founded Nalanda as a small Buddhist monastery. By the time of Xuanzang's visit more than 800 years later, it had grown into the largest university of its time. Xuanzang describes it as an awesome and beautiful place: "One gate opens into the great college, from which

Xuanzang, *A Record of the Western Regions*, seventh century CE

Historians believe this may be a painting of Xuanzang carrying his beloved Buddhist scriptures. It is from a Buddhist cave temple in Dunhuang, a major stop on the Silk Road, which led from India to China.

are separated eight other walls, standing in the middle. The richly adorned towers, and the fairy-like turrets, like painted hilltops; are congregated together. The observatories seem to be lost in the mist, and the upper rooms tower above the clouds."

Buddhist kings and wealthy merchants all over Asia supported the university. The king of Burma sent ships filled with jewels to pay for restoring the buildings in the tenth century. Buddhists could study there for free, and non-Buddhists either paid a fee or worked for the university as

NOW THAT'S DETERMINATION

The story goes that soon after he had left China, Xuanzang realized he was lost and without water. He looked back and saw the last Chinese watchtower in the distance. For a moment, he was tempted to return. But then he remembered that he had taken an oath that he would rather die facing west than live in the east. So he pressed on. Not long afterward, his horse left the path and would not return. Xuanzang thought he was lost for sure. But his horse had smelled water, and a few minutes later he staggered into an oasis that saved their lives.

THE SILK ROAD AND OTHER TRADE ROUTES, 300 BCE—500 CE

IT'S HARD TO SAY NO TO A KING

One of the reasons Xuanzang's journey took so long is that he was not the only Buddhist who wanted to learn more about his faith. The Buddhist king of the oasis at Turfan was typical. He was so excited about having someone who could teach him more about the Buddha that he wouldn't let Xuanzang out of his city gates (that were in the shape of giant Buddhas). Finally, Xuanzang stopped eating until he was allowed to leave.

laborers. Xuanzang later wrote that the entrance exams were so difficult that only about one out of every five foreign students who applied was admitted.

At Nalanda, Xuanzang studied Buddhist scripture such as the *Tripitakas*, the *Sutras*, and the *Jataka Tales*, stories of the Buddha and his previous lives. At some point in his studies, he may have visited the Ajanta caves, whose painted walls taught Buddhist scripture in a slightly different way. Like Nalanda, the caves at Ajanta were first a monastery and then became a kind of Buddhist university. But the caves at Ajanta stored images, not just books. Like a stained glass window in a medieval European cathedral, the walls of the caves were filled with pictures of sacred stories painted by the monks. Many of the painted stories came from the *Jataka Tales* and they were meant to teach people about the Buddha, just as the stories in medieval stained glass were meant to teach Christians about Christ.

The walls of the caves were covered with a strong plaster made of lime that coated the rough rock surface and made a smooth, tight canvas. After the plaster was dry, the monk-artist would sketch in his subject with a charcoal pencil. Then he would paint the outlines, fill them in with base colors, and let that dry. Finally he would add shading and details.

If Xuanzang were a scholar visiting the caves at Ajanta today, he would probably not be studying Buddhism, but life at the Gupta court. The paintings show us the simple clothing styles and elaborate jewelry that people wore in Gupta times. They also tell us that the people of the Gupta age believed that beauty helped people learn about spiritual things.

Gupta temples were also places of beauty. The Guptas believed that when they were in a temple, the gap between

Rows of buddhas meditating on the walls of the Ajanta cave in India represent the Buddha teaching at the city of Sravasti, where he multiplied himself hundreds of times to show the power of his teachings.

them and their gods was closed. They built their temples with designs that followed strict rules. Temples faced east, into the rising sun. A series of gates and entrance halls helped people to orient themselves to the order of the universe. At last the worshippers arrived at the center of the temple, called the "sacred womb." From there, the only direction is up, through the umbrella-shaped spire to the heavens.

Xuanzang wrote that "The rafters and roof beams [of temples] are carved with strange figures, and the doors, windows and walls are painted in various colors." The "strange figures" were statues of the gods, which were made

Xuanzang, *A Record of the Western Regions*, seventh century CE

This chaitya, or chapel, is from one of a series of Buddhist caves in Ajanta, India. The seated image of the Buddha and a domed stupa with the ashes of the Buddha or a saint would have been the focus of worship.

from stone, wood, metal, plaster, painting, sand, and jewels. These statues were either "fixed"—part of the temple—or "movable," which meant they could be picked up and used in religious parades and processions. The gods were invited to live in the "fixed" statues full time, but were invited to enter the "movable" statues only when these were used for worship. (That's why it's okay for children to play with figurines that were first made for worship—the god left when the worship was done.)

The *Puranas*, a collection of Hindu myths, explain how people should worship the statues (the "Me" is the statue):

> When offering Me the bath with fragrant water, the Vedic mantras...should be recited. With clothes, sacred thread, jewels, garlands, and fragrant paste, My devotee should decorate my form suitably and with love. With faith, My worshiper should then offer Me water to wash, sandal, flower, unbroken rice, incense, light, and food of different kinds; also attentions like anointing, massage, showing of mirror, etc., and entertainments like song and dance; these special attentions and entertainments may be done of festive days and even daily.

Bhagavata Purana, 800–1000 CE

The rules about carving a statue were very strict. The forehead should be broad like that of an elephant and the arms and legs slender and smooth like the trunk of a banana tree. The hands and feet should be like a lotus, with long slender fingers like the bean pod. The position of each part of the body had special meaning, especially the hands. Hand positions, called *mudras*, were also important in Indian dance and drama.

After 13 years of study, Xuanzang decided that he had learned enough, and he started the long journey back to China, carrying 657 Buddhist texts written on paper and palm leaves and some astonishing memories of the greatness of Gupta culture. A new emperor was on the Chinese throne, and he was eager to hear all that he could about the glory of India. This new emperor didn't care that Xuanzang had broken the ban on foreign travel.

RELIGIOUS WRITINGS OF SOUTH ASIA

Vedas	*Oldest Hindu scriptures. The earliest is the* Rig Veda, *a collection of hymns. The most recent are the Upanishads, which can only be learned with the help of a teacher.*
Puranas	*The Vedas-made-easy, for ordinary people who did not have time for study. Also described as Hindu myths*
Mahabharata, including Bhagavad Gita	*Beloved Hindu poem about Prince Arjuna*
Ramayana	*The story of Prince Rama and his beautiful wife Sita*
Jatakas	*Stories about the Buddha's previous lives that explain karma, or the law of consequences*
Panchatantra	*Many of these are animal stories for children*
Tripitaka	*Buddhist sermons and teachings*
Sutras	*Mahayana Buddhist sermons. The most famous is the Lotus Sutra, which explains the idea of a bodhisattva, or teacher*

When his curious countrymen asked him about the wonders Xuanzang had seen, he was polite, but he made it clear that he had gone to find the word of the Buddha—not to be corrupted by the lavish art, music, dance, and drama of the Gupta court. But the emperor wanted to know everything about Gupta culture, and finally Xuanzang agreed to write a book—just one: *A Record of the Western Regions*— about what he had seen. When he finished the book, Xuanzang took his Buddhist manuscripts and spent the rest of his life translating them from Sanskrit into Chinese, happy to have the word of the Buddha at last.

EPILOGUE

THE LEGACY OF ANCIENT SOUTH ASIA

66 **KALIDASA AND RAMAPRASAD**

Today, the peoples of South Asia live in seven major countries: India, Pakistan, Afghanistan, Nepal, Bangladesh, Sri Lanka, and Bhutan. Each country has its history, customs, and habits of worship. Although many things have changed over time, one thing that remains as true today as in the past is that "the people are fond of festivity." In India, most people are Hindu. They worship gods and goddesses such as Krishna, Shiva, and Kali. They believe that a person's spirit doesn't die, but is reborn into a new life. And, until recently, Indians believed that society should be divided into castes.

66 Kalidasa, *Shakuntala*, fifth– sixth century CE

But not everyone in South Asia is Hindu. Some, like most Nepalis, are Buddhist. Some are Muslim. Muslims follow the teachings of the prophet Muhammad, who was born in an oasis town in Arabia in 570 CE. Muslims believe that when Muhammad was a young man, an angel appeared to him and told him that there was one god, Allah, and no other god but Allah. The angel emphasized that followers of Allah must never make any images of him, because they might worship

This image of the goddess Durga is made of bamboo, clay, and paper for the annual festival for the goddess. At the end of the celebration, it will be placed in the Ganga River to dissolve.

A bearded musician plays a stringed instrument similar to the rabab, which is still played throughout Afghanistan and northern Pakistan. The robed woman plays the cymbals.

WE REALLY MEAN WORLD MUSIC

One of South Asia's most popular musical instruments is called the sitar. It is based on the *veena*, a boat-shaped instrument that the goddess Saraswati plays, combined with instruments from Persia and the Middle East. The name comes from the Persian word *sehtar*—meaning "seven strings." The modern sitar has 5 main melody strings, 2 rhythm strings, and 11 strings used for harmony. A musician plucks the strings with a *mizrab*, a wire pick worn on the tip of the index finger.

Ancient paintings show people playing the sitar during religious festivals. After the Muslims came to South Asia, the sitar became a popular instrument at the Mughal court. Over the last few decades, more and more musicians who enjoy international music have begun to play and listen to the sitar.

the images instead of Allah himself. Those beliefs have made it hard for Muslims and Hindus to agree. During the Middle Ages, Muslim armies conquered India. Today, most Pakistanis and citizens of Bangladesh are Muslim.

South Asia is a startlingly diverse place. Many of its inhabitants are vegetarian, like the Jains, and many agree with Buddhism's Four Noble Truths. Greek culture and Persian religion and ideas about government are also part of South Asia's history, as are the words, foods, and customs of traders from Portugal, Africa, China, Britain, and Indonesia. It can be hard to agree on anything, even a way to greet each other. The British shook hands, but many South Asians are uncomfortable touching each other. Hindus show respect by putting their hands together and bowing their heads, just as they have done for 4,500 years. Muslim communities raise their right hands to their foreheads and then place them over their hearts. But somehow, in most places and at most times, the differences make life more interesting.

Sometimes a single event or celebration works for everyone—in different ways. Take Divali, India's festival of lights, which is celebrated for four days in the late fall. For Hindus who worship Vishnu and his avatar Rama, Divali is a celebration of when Rama became king. For history buffs, Divali marks when Chandra Gupta II became king. For wealthy merchant communities in Western India, Divali is the beginning of their new year and a time to worship Lakshmi, the goddess of wealth. They paint their houses, shops, and offices. They open new account books and start everything fresh. They decorate their homes with simple oil lamps or glittering electric lights, give sweets to children, and set off fireworks.

In northern India, Divali celebrates the end of the southwest monsoon and the time when the god Vishnu destroyed the demon Naraka. In this part of the country, people end Divali by burning a big paper image of the demon. But in southern India, Divali is the time for *worshipping* a demon king. According to local traditions, Vishnu conquered the local demon king Bali, and then banished him from his kingdom to live forever in the netherworld. Bali begged Vishnu to allow him to return for one day each year to visit his land and the people he greatly loved. For ten days, people celebrate the end of the harvest by singing songs about their beloved king, feasting, and giving each other presents, especially new clothes.

Another of India's popular festivals celebrates the powerful goddess Durga, also known as Kali and Lakshmi. In the 18th century CE, the Bengali poet Ramaprasad wrote, "O my mind, I tell you, worship Kali the Divine Mother, in whatever fashion you desire." When demons defeated the

❝ Ramaprasad, 18th century CE

A terracotta tablet from Harappa shows the ritual slaying of a water buffalo in front of a god seated in yogic position, while a crocodile crawls above the scene. Today, the crocodile and water buffalo sacrifices are associated with the goddess Durga; these modern beliefs may have had their roots in the Indus civilization.

A boy sells chutneys (relishes) and achars (pickles) at market in Pakistan. Flavor and variety are important to South Asian cooking—and South Asian life.

gods, the goddess Durga appeared, her golden skin glowing like the sun. She fought the demons for seven days, finally destroying a demon called the "Water Buffalo Demon of Ignorance." On the eighth day, she went among the people of the land and encouraged them to have a victory feast—where a water buffalo was sacrificed.

In many regions, people worship Durga for the first three nights, then worship the goddess in the form of Lakshmi, the goddess of wealth, for the next three. During the last three days, they worship Saraswati, the goddess of learning and music, by putting books, writing tools, and musical instruments on her altar for her to bless.

After nine nights of worship, people parade to a nearby river or lake carrying brightly decorated images of Durga made of clay, paper and bamboo. They leave the images, which are made of papier-mâché or unfired clay, to dissolve in the water. That has been the proper way to dispose of sacred images for thousands of years.

Durga is a powerful goddess. Because she is called the "Goddess of War who fights Evil," Durga was also worshipped by Hindu revolutionaries who wanted to overthrow outside conquerors—first Arabs, Turks, and Persians and then the British in the 19th century.

Festivals just wouldn't be festivals without lots of food. As with its art and religious beliefs, South Asia's food has been influenced by many people and places. The most common dish is called a *kari*, often translated as "curry." Not surprisingly, "curry" means different things in the different parts in South Asia. Traditional curry is a mild sauce made with yoghurt and spices, sometimes mixed with vegetables. During the British colonial period, from 1766 to 1947, the word "curry" came to be applied to all dishes with a thick spicy sauce. The basic spices in curry powder are coriander, cumin, turmeric, and fenugreek. Hot spices such as black pepper and ginger, and aromatic spices such as cinnamon, cardamom, nutmeg, and cloves, are added for variety. Black pepper and ginger were the hot spices in ancient times. The chili pepper didn't arrive in South Asia until after the 1500s—now it's an important part of the South Asian cooking. Still, South Asian cooking is not so much "hot and spicy" as it is "flavorful spicy."

It's really hard to sum up a place that is as diverse and rich in history as South Asia. It's like a flavorful curry, served with lots of chutneys and achars on the side—sometimes sweet, sometimes sour, but always colorful and exciting.

I'M IN A REAL ACHAR

A South Asian meal sparks the taste buds with a blend of different flavors. A traditional meal can have up to 16 different dishes, including chutneys and achars. Chutney, served cold or hot, is a fresh relish made with vegetables or fruit mixed with spices and other ingredients to make it sweet, hot, tangy, sour, or bitter. Achars are pickles packed in spices and oil and are spicier than chutneys. Chutneys and achars spark the taste buds and add variety and flavor to the main dishes.

TIMELINE

The centuries BCE and CE are mirror images of each other. The years go backwards before the year 1 CE. So someone born in 2000 BCE who died in 1935 BCE would have lived to be 65 years old. On both sides of the "mirror," the 200s can also be called the 3rd century, the 900s are called the 10th century, and so on—BCE as well as CE.

BCE

7000
Neolithic era; agriculture begins in the Indus Valley; craftspeople make stone beads and shell bangles in Mehrgarh

5500
Artisans make pottery and copper and bronze tools in Mehrgarh

4500
Potters make identification marks on pottery

3900
Stone beads and shell bangles used in Harappa

3500
Potters' wheels used at Mehrgarh

3300
Early writing at Harappa

2800–2600
Early Harappan period; first mud-brick city walls built

2600–1900
Indus Valley civilization develops; Harappan period; large, planned cities emerge throughout the Indus region

2600
Villagers of Harappa and Mohenjo Daro build drains and baked-brick houses

1900–1300
Indus cities decline

1700–1500
Rig Veda, the oldest part of the Vedas, compiled

1500–1200
Earliest use of iron and horses in South Asia

1500–800
Vedic communities spread from Indus to Ganga River valley; the later Vedas, a collection of hymns, mantras, and religious instructions, compiled

1000–600
Early Hindu epic poems *Mahabharata* and *Ramayana* are first composed

700–500
Brahmin influence, the foundation of later Hinduism, spreads throughout northern subcontinent

600–500
Buddhism and Jainism (nonviolence) emerge

558–529
Persians invade under Cyrus the Great

Between 420–350
Buddha dies and attains Nirvana

Between 400–300
Kautilya writes *Arthashastra*

327–325
Greeks invade under Alexander the Great

326
Alexander and Porus wage battle, ending in a truce and friendship

325
Alexander and most of his army leave the Indus Valley and return to Babylon

321–297
Chandragupta Maurya reigns

302
Megasthenes, ambassador of Selukos, visits court of Chandragupta Maurya

269–232
Ashoka reigns

261
Ashoka supports Buddhism

200 BCE–200 CE
Buddhist influence reaches its height

185
Mauryan dynasty ends

50 BCE–150 CE
Kushana invade and Kanishka rules; Gandhara art flourishes; Buddhism splits into several sects

CE

200–300
Laws of Manu are codified

250
Sanskrit literature develops

320–335
Chandra Gupta I reigns

320–540
Gupta era; arts and
sciences flourish
and *Panchatantra*
written

335–376
Samudra Gupta
reigns

376–415
Chandra Gupta II reigns

About 400
Kalidasa, Sanskrit poet and writer, active

405–411
Fa Hien visits India

415–455
Kumara Gupta reigns

454
White Huns first invade, destroy religious
centers and major cities

455–467
Skanda Gupta reigns, defeats the first Hun
invaders

476–550
Astronomer Aryabhata active

495
White Huns invade once again, establish
small kingdoms in the north

580–632
Prophet Muhammad lives

595
Earliest use of zero

630–643
Xuanzang
visits India

712
Arabs occupy
Sindh;
introduction
of Islam to
South Asia

FURTHER READING

Entries with 66 *indicate primary source material.*

GENERAL WORKS ON ANCIENT SOUTH ASIA

Allchin, Bridget. *Origins of a Civilization: The Prehistory and Early Archaeology of South Asia.* New York: Viking, 1997.

Allchin, Raymond, ed. *The Archaeology of Early Historic South Asia: The Emergence of Cities and States.* New York: Cambridge University Press, 1995.

Auboyer, Jeannine. *Daily Life in Ancient India: From 200 BC to 700 AD.* Translated by Watson Taylor. London: Phoenix, 2002.

Basham, A. L. *The Wonder that Was India.* New York: Grove, 1967.

The Editors of Time-Life. *Ancient India: Land of Mystery.* Alexandria, Va.: Time-Life Books, 1994.

Einfeld, Jann. *India.* San Diego, Calif.: Greenhaven, 2003.

Keay, John. *India: A History,* rev. ed. New York: HarperCollins, 2001.

Sundaram, T. R. "Ancient Jewel." *The World & I.* Oct. 1996.

Wolpert, Stanley. *A New History of India.* 7th ed. New York: Oxford University Press, 2003.

ATLASES AND GEOGRAPHY

Barter, James. *The Ganges.* San Diego, Calif.: Greenhaven, 2002.

Haywood, John. *World Atlas of the Past: Vol. 1: The Ancient World.* New York: Oxford University Press, 1999.

Johnson, Gordon. *Cultural Atlas of India: India, Pakistan, Nepal, Bhutan, Bangladesh & Sri Lanka.* New York: Facts on File, 1996.

Mountjoy, Shane. *Indus River.* New York: Chelsea House, 2005.

ENCYCLOPEDIA

Lochtefeld, James. *The Illustrated Encyclopedia of Hinduism,* vol. 2, New York: Rosen Publishing Group, 2001.

BIOGRAPHY

"Akbar of India." *Calliope.* March 2005.

"Ashoka, India's Philosopher King." *Calliope.* January 2000.

Demi. *Buddha.* New York: Henry Holt, 1996.

ART AND ARCHITECTURE

Aruz, Joan, ed. *The Art of the First Cities: The Third Millennium BC from the Mediterranean to the Indus.* New Haven, Conn.: Yale University Press, 2003.

Dehejia, Vidya. *Indian Art.* London: Phaidon Press, 1997.

Huntington, Susan L. *Art of Ancient India.* Boston, Mass.: Weatherhill, 1985.

Kossack, Steven M., and Edith W. Watts. *The Art of South and Southeast Asia: A Resource for Educators.* New York: Metropolitan Museum of Art, 2001.

INDUS VALLEY CIVILIZATION

Aronovsky, Ilona, and Sujata Gopinath. *The Indus Valley.* Chicago: Heinemann, 2005.

Kenoyer, Jonathan Mark. *Ancient Cities of the Indus Valley Civilization.* New York: Oxford University Press, 1998.

Kenoyer, J. M. "Uncovering the keys to the Lost Indus Cities." *Scientific American* July 2003, 67–75.

Kirkpatrick, Naida. *The Indus Valley.* Chicago: Heinemann, 2002.

Menon, Shanti. "Indus Valley, Inc." *Discover* December 1998; 67–71.

LITERATURE AND MYTHS

[66] Alphonso-Karkala, John B., ed. *An Anthology of Indian Literature*, 2nd ed. Noida, India: Penguin/Indian Council for Cultural Relations, 1987.

[66] Daniélou, Alain. *The Myths and Gods of India*. Rochester, Vt.: Inner Traditions International, 1991.

[66] ———. *Shilappadikaram (The Ankle Bracelet) by Prince Illango Adigal*. New York: New Directions, 1965.

[66] Gray, J. E. B, and Rosamund Fowler. *Tales from India*. rev. ed. New York: Oxford University Press, 2001.

[66] Jaffrey, Madhur, and Michael Foreman. *Seasons of Splendour: Tales, Myths, and Legends of India*. New York: Viking, 1992.

[66] Laya, K. *India: World Myths and Legends*. Upper Saddle River, N.J.: Globe Fearon, 1992.

[66] Miller, Barbara Stoller, trans. *The Bhagavad Gita: Krishna's Counsel in Times of War*. New York: Bantam, 1986.

[66] Narayan, R. K. *Mahabharata: A Shortened Modern Prose Version of the Indian Epic*. Chicago: University of Chicago Press, 2000.

[66] ———. *Ramayana: A Shortened Modern Prose Version of the Indian Epic*. New York: Penguin, 1998.

RELIGION

"Buddhism." *Calliope*. March/ April 1995.

Champakalakshmi, R. *The Hindu Temple*. New Delhi: Roli & Janssen BV, 2001

Ganeri, Anita. *The Ramayana and Hinduism*. Mankato, Minn: Smart Apple Media, 2003.

MacMillan, Dianne M. *Diwali: Hindu Festival of Lights*. Berkeley Heights, N.J.: Enslow, 1997.

Wilkinson, Phillip. *Buddhism*. New York: Dorling Kindersley, 2001.

SCIENCE AND TECHNOLOGY

Chattopadhyaya, Debiprasad. *History of Science and Technology in Ancient India: Astronomy, Science, and Society*. Columbia, Mo.: South Asia Books, 1996.

Stewart, Melissa. *Science in Ancient India*. London: Franklin Watts: 1999.

VEDIC AND EARLY HINDU SOUTH ASIA

Bowden, Rob, and Richard Spilsbury. *Settlements of the Ganges River*. Heinemann, 2004.

Hinds, Kathryn. *India's Gupta Dynasty*. New York: Benchmark Books, 1996.

"India's Gupta Dynasty." *Calliope*. November 2002.

Dallapiccola, Anna L. *Dictionary of Hindu Lore and Legend*. London: Thames and Hudson, 2002.

WEBSITES

INDEX

TEXT CREDITS

MAIN TEXT

P. 21: R. K. Narayan. *The Ramayana: A Shortened Modern Prose Version.* New York: Penguin, 1977, 117.

P. 28: M. A. Stein, trans. *Kalhana's Rajatarangini: A Chronicle of the Kings of Kashmir.* Delhi: Motilal Banarsidas, 1961, 388–89.

P. 65: H. E. W. Crawford. "Mesopotamia's Invisible Exports in the Third Millennium B.C." *World Archaeology* 5 (2): 232–41.

P. 69: Narayan, *The Ramayana,* 118.

P. 72: Dinesh Agrawal, trans. *Rig Veda. www.hindunet.org/hindu_history/ancient/aryan/aryan_agrawal.html,* VII, 95.

P. 75: Agrawal, trans., *Rig Veda.*

P. 80: Frits Staal, ed. *Agni: The Vedic Ritual of the Fire Alter,* Vol. 2. Berkeley, Calif.: Asian Humanities Press, 1983. Plate 49, RV 3,27.1;6.16.10.

P. 82: Barbara Stoller Miller, trans. *The Bhagavad Gita: Krishna's Counsel in Times of War.* New York: Bantam, 1986, II, 7.

P. 83: Miller, trans., *The Bhagavad Gita,* IX, 3, 18.

P. 84: Miller, trans., *The Bhagavad Gita,* I, 19.

P. 85: Narayan, *The Ramayana,* 158.

P. 87: Narayan, *The Ramayana,* 158.

P. 88: Shanti Lal Nagar. *Brahmavaivarta Purana.* Delhi: Parimal Publications, 2001, 563.

P. 90: Narayan, *The Ramayana,* 90.

Alain Daniélou. *The Myths and Gods of India.* Rochester, Vt.: Inner Traditions International, 1991, 198.

P. 93: Narayan, *The Ramayana,* 164.

P. 97: John B. Alphonso-Karkala, ed. *An Anthology of Indian Literature,* 2nd ed. Noida, India: Penguin/Indian Council for Cultural Relations, 1987, 187.

P. 100: William T. De Bary, ed. *Sources of Indian Tradition,* Vol. 1. New York: Columbia University Press, 1958, 122.

Alphonso-Karkala, ed. *An Anthology of Indian Literature,* 216–20.

P. 102: De Bary, ed. *Sources of Indian Tradition,* 144.

P. 104: Richard Salomon. *Indian Epigraphy: A guide to the Study of Inscriptions in Sanskrit, Prakrit, and the Other Indo-Aryan Languages.* New York: Oxford University Press, 1998, 207.

P. 107: R. Chalmers. *The Jataka or Stories for the Buddha's Former Births,* Vol 1. London: Luzac, 1957, 193–94.

P. 110: McCrindle, *The Invasion of India by Alexander the Great,* 92.

P. 113: B. Prakash, *Poros the Great.* Lahore: Gautam Press, 1994, 75.

McCrindle, *The Invasion of India by Alexander the Great,* 109.

P. 114: L. N. Rangarajan, ed. *Kautilya: The Arthashastra.* New Delhi: Penguin, 1992, 377.

P. 115: Rangarajan, ed. *Kautilya,* 183.

P. 118: S. Balachandra Rao. *Indian Mathematics and Astronomy: Some Landmarks.* Bangalore: Jnana Deep Publications, 1994, 47, 31.

P. 122: Hemchandra Raychaudhuri. *Political History of Ancient India: From the Accession of Parikshit to the Extinction of the Gupta Dynasty.* Calcutta: University of Calcutta, 1953, 270.

P. 123: S. Dhammika, trans. "An English Rendering of the Edicts of Asoka." In *Asoka 2300: Jagajjyoti: Asoka Commemoration Volume 1997 A.D./2541 B.E.,* edited by H. B. Chowdhury. Calcutta: The Bengal Buddhist Association, 1997, 52.

P. 124: Dhammika, trans., "An English Rendering of the Edicts of Asoka," 52, 53.

P. 126: Alain Daniélou. *Shilappadikaram (The Ankle Bracelet) by Prince Illango Adigal.* New York: New Directions Books, 1965, 105–06.

P. 127: Daniélou, trans., *Shilappadikaram (The Ankle Bracelet),* 106.

P. 128: Daniélou, trans., *Shilappadikaram (The Ankle Bracelet),* 143.

P. 129: Santosh Kumar Das. *The Educational System of the Ancient Hindus.* Calcutta: G. B. Manna, Mitra Press, 1930.

Das, *The Educational System of the Ancient Hindus,* 223.

P. 130: Patrick Olivelle *The Law Code of Manu: A New Translation.* New York: Oxford University Press, 2004, 35.

P. 139: Olivelle, *The Law Code of Manu,* 21.

P. 140: Olivelle, *The Law Code of Manu,* 96.

P. 141: Olivelle, *The Law Code of Manu,* 156–57.

V. Mitra. *Education in Ancient India.* New Delhi: Arya Book Depot, 1964, 9.

P. 142: Olivelle, *The Law Code of Manu,* 95.

P. 144: R. N. Saletore. *Life in the Gupta Age.* Bombay: The Popular Book Depot, 1943, 253–54.

P. 146: Rajbali Pandey. *Chandragupta II Vikramaditya.* Varanasi: Chaukhamba Amarabharati Prakashan, 1982, 75.

P. 147: Beal, *Chinese Acounts of India,* 240.

Rama Shankar Tripathi. *History of Ancient India.* Delhi: Motilal Banarsidas, 1942, 280.

P. 148: Beal, *Chinese Acounts of India,* 99, 86.

Saletore, *Life in the Gupta Age,* 572–73.

P. 152–53: Saletore, *Life in the Gupta Age,* 171–72.

P. 153: De Bary, ed. *Sources of India Tradition,* 336.

P. 157: De Bary, ed. *Sources of India Tradition,* 359.

SIDEBARS

P. 22: J. W. McCrindle, ed. *The Invasion of India by Alexander the Great as Described by Arrian, Q. Curtius, Diodoros, Plutarch and Justin.* New York: Barnes and Noble, 1969, 96.

P. 86: Narayan, *The Ramayana,* 148.

P. 96: Sir Edwin Arnold, trans. *Bhagavad Gita.* Mineola, N.Y.: Dover, 1993, VI, 70.

P. 120: Swami Satya Prakash. *Founders of Sciences in Ancient India.* New Delhi: The Research Institute of Ancient Scientific Studies, 1965, 270–71.

P. 143: Sarla Khosla. *Gupta Civilization.* New Delhi: Intellectual Publishing House, 1982, 109–10.

P. 144: Beal, S. *Chinese Accounts of India: Translated from the Chinese of Hiuen Tsiang,* Vol. 2. Calcutta: Susil Gupta, 1958, 21.

PICTURE CREDITS

ACKNOWLEDGMENTS

The authors would like to first thank the peoples and cultures of South Asia for providing such a stimulating subject to write about. We hope that this book serves to honor the ancient cultures and modern peoples of this great region. We also are forever indebted to Oxford University Press for bringing us together as co-authors. This experience has taught us both to appreciate different ways of teaching and writing about the past. We wish to thank Ron Mellor and Amanda Podany for making this project possible and lending us both their considerable expertise and moral support along the way. We'd also like to thank our editors at Oxford, Karen Fein, Nancy Toff, and Nancy Hirsch, for their patience and their help in making this complex topic more accessible to young readers.

Jonathan Mark Kenoyer would especially like to thank the Department of Archaeology and Museums, Government of Pakistan and the Archaeological Survey of India, Government of India, and all of the archaeologists and students who have made it possible for him to work in both countries. He would also like to specifically thank the many funding agencies who provided him support during his many years of research: the National Science Foundation, the National Endowment for the Humanities, the National Geographic Society, the Smithsonian Institution, American Schools of Prehistoric Research (Peabody Museum of Harvard University), the Fulbright Foundation, University of Wisconsin and Harvard University, and many private donors.

Finally, we are grateful to a number of individuals for providing information and practical assistance at crucial junctures. Kenoyer would like to especially thank his Sanskrit teacher Dr. Robert Goldman and his archaeology professor the late George F. Dales for helping him get started in this long study of ancient South Asia. He also would like to thank Dr. Richard Meadow and Dr. Rita Wright, and all his archaeological colleagues from the Harappa Archaeological Research Project, as well as Dr. Jean François and Catherine Jarrige from the French Archaeological Mission to Pakistan for their contributions to the study of the ancient Indus culture. A special thanks to Mr. Jamil Bhatti from Shorkot for sharing his knowledge and enthusiasm for the past. Kimberly Heuston would like to thank Sandra Camargo, Nancy and Dusty Heuston, and Heather Rosett.

JONATHAN MARK KENOYER is professor of anthropology at the University of Wisconsin at Madison, where he has taught since 1985. He was born and raised in India, speaks several South Asian languages fluently, and has a deep love for the subcontinent. He has a B.A. in anthropology from the University of California at Berkeley and completed his M.A. and Ph.D. in South Asian archaeology from the same university. His main focus is on the Indus Valley civilization, but he also has experience with the Paleolithic period and historical archaeology and ethnoarchaeology. He has conducted archaeological research and excavations at both Mohenjo Daro and Harappa, two of the most important Indus-period sites in Pakistan. He has a special interest in ancient technologies and crafts and socio-economic and political organization as well as religion. He has written many books and articles, including *Ancient Cities of the Indus Valley.*

KIMBERLEY HEUSTON writes historical fiction for young adults and teaches English and history at the Waterford School in Sandy, Utah. Raised in New York City, where she attended the Spence School, Ms. Heuston graduated from Harvard University in 1981 with a degree in history and science. Her teaching honors include summer fellowships sponsored by the Esther A. and Joseph Klingenstein Fund, the Woodrow Wilson Center, the National Endowment for the Humanities, and the Fulbright Commission. She received an M.F.A. in writing for children from Vermont College in 2000. Her novels include *The Shakeress, Dante's Daughter,* and *The Velvet Years.* She is the mother of four children, one of whom has the good fortune to be married to Natalie.

RONALD MELLOR, who is professor of history at UCLA, first became enthralled with ancient history as a student at Regis High School in New York City. He is the statewide faculty advisor of the California History–Social Science Project (CHSSP), which brings university faculty together with K-12 teachers at sites throughout California. In 2000, the American Historical Association awarded the CHSSP the Albert J. Beveridge Award for K-12 teaching. Professor Mellor has held fellowships from the National Endowment for the Humanities and the American Council of Learned Societies. His research has centered on ancient religion and Roman historiography. His books include *Theia Rhome: The Goddess Roma in the Greek World, From Augustus to Nero: The First Dynasty of Imperial Rome, Tacitus, Tacitus: The Classical Heritage, The Historians of Ancient Rome, The Roman Historians,* and *The Ancient Roman World* (with Marni McGee), also in The World in Ancient Times series.

AMANDA H. PODANY is a specialist in the history of the Ancient Near East and a professor of history at California State Polytechnic University, Pomona. She has taught there since 1990 and is currently serving as the director of the university's honors program. From 1993 to 1997 she was executive director of the California History–Social Science Project, a professional development program for history–social science teachers at all grade levels. Her publications include *The Land of Hana: Kings, Chronology, Scribal Tradition* and *The Ancient Near Eastern World* (with Marni McGee), also in The World in Ancient Times series. Professor Podany has also published numerous journal articles on ancient Near Eastern history and on approaches to teaching. She lives in Los Angeles with her husband and two children.